PROBLEMS AND EXEI
FOR
INTERMEDIATE MICROECONOMICS

Frank Westhoff
Amherst College

To accompany
INTERMEDIATE MICROECONOMICS
AND ITS APPLICATION
Eighth Edition

Walter Nicholson
Amherst College

THE DRYDEN PRESS
Chicago   New York   San Francisco
Philadelphia   Montreal   Toronto
London   Sydney   Tokyo

ISBN: 0-03-025918-5

Address for Domestic Orders
Harcourt College Publishers, 6277 Sea Harbor Drive, Orlando, FL 32887-6777
800-782-4479

Address for International Orders
International Customer Service
Harcourt, Inc., 6277 Sea Harbor Drive, Orlando, FL 32887-6777
407-345-3800
(fax) 407-345-4060
(e-mail) hbintl@harcourt.com

Address for Editorial Correspondence
Harcourt College Publishers, 301 Commerce Street, Suite 3700, Fort Worth, TX 76102

Web Site Address
http://www.harcourtcollege.com

Printed in the United States of America

0 1 2 3 4 5 6 7 8 9   023   11 10 9 8 7 6 5 4 3 2

Harcourt College Publishers

INTRODUCTION

This Study Guide will help you understand the material presented in *Intermediate Microeconomics and Its Application*, 8/e, by Walter Nicholson. It contains four elements to help you grasp the concepts presented in the textbook: learning objectives, walking tour summaries, multiple-choice questions, and running glossaries. Each walking tour summary and running glossary omits key words and replaces them with blanks. After studying a chapter, you should write the missing key words in the blanks in the left-hand margin. Also, you should answer the multiple-choice questions in the same manner. The answers appear at the end of each chapter.

I designed the Study Guide to keep you actively involved. You cannot simply skim through the following pages paying little attention to the material. You must continuously fill in the blanks. We hope that by being an active participant, rather than a passive spectator, you will learn the material faster and more thoroughly.

Frank Westhoff

TABLE OF CONTENTS

PART 1

INTRODUCTION

CHAPTER 1

ECONOMIC MODELS

LEARNING OBJECTIVES

- Economic models describe the essential aspects of the economy.
- The demand and supply curves illustrate the equilibrium price and quantity of a single good in a competitive market.
- A partial equilibrium model focuses on a single market, on the price and quantity of a single good.
- A general equilibrium model focuses on interrelationships of markets.

WALKING TOUR SUMMARIES

ECONOMIC MODELS

1. _____ _____ exists because there are not enough productive resources available to satisfy all human wants. There is not enough land, labor, and capital to produce all the food, clothing, automobiles, furniture, etc. that we

2. _____ human beings would like to consume. _____ studies the allocation of scarce resources among alternative end uses. Economists strive to understand how decisions to use land, labor, and capital in alternative productive processes

3. _____ are made. _____ is the study of the economic choices individuals and firms make.

   Real-world economies are very complex. Every day thousands of firms and millions of households make thousands of millions of decisions. These decisions affect the allocation of scarce resources among alternative productive processes. It is impossible to describe all these decisions in complete detail; so, economists make _____ _____ assumptions to formulate models.

4. _____

SUPPLY AND DEMAND: THE DEVELOPMENT OF AN ECONOMIC MODEL

In *The Wealth of Nations*, Adam Smith first observed that the pattern of market-determined prices provided a powerful "invisible hand" to direct resources into activities where they are _____ valuable. Smith's explanation of how prices are determined proved only partially correct, however. Smith argued that a good's cost of production determines its price. David Ricardo recognized that Smith's view of price determination was incomplete. He introduced the law of _____ marginal returns. As more and more of a good is produced the additional cost associated with the production of one more unit _____. Both Smith and Ricardo only considered production when explaining prices.

5. _____

6. _____

7. _____

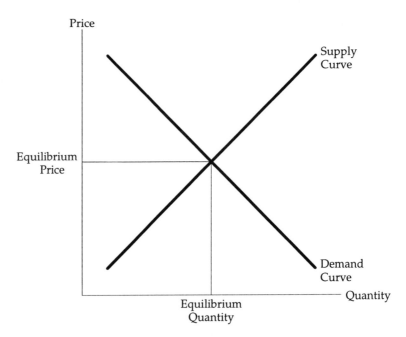

Figure 1.1: *Demand and Supply Curves*

Alfred Marshall extended Ricardo's notion of marginalism to include not only production, but also _____. He recognized that the _____ unit consumed and produced determines a good's value. As we consume more

8. _____

9. _____

10. _____
11. _____
12. _____

13. _____

14. _____

15. _____
16. _____

and more of a good, we are not willing to pay as much for the _____ unit. That is, *marginal usefulness* _____ and the demand curve slopes _____. On the other hand, as firms produce more and more of a good the change in total cost required to produce one additional unit _____. That is, *marginal cost* increases and the supply curve slopes _____. The demand and supply curves together determine a good's exchange value. The intersection of the demand and supply curves illustrates the _____ price. This is a(n) _____ equilibrium model because it depicts the determination of a single good's price.

MODELS OF MANY MARKETS

17. _____

18. _____

A(n) _____ equilibrium model describes the interrelationship of the markets for all goods. The *production possibility curve* illustrates all the combinations of goods that can be produced from a fixed amount of resources. The production possibility curve slopes _____, reflecting the opportunity cost of each good. The production possibility curve illustrates how much of one good must be sacrificed to produce more of another good.

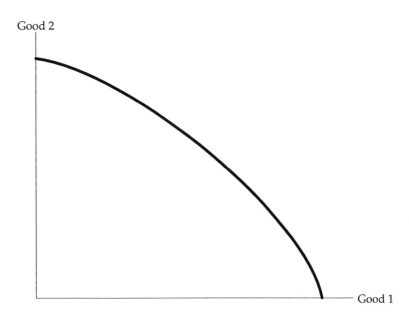

Figure 1.2: *Production Possibility Curve*

HOW ECONOMISTS VERIFY THEORETICAL MODELS

19. _____

20. _____

21. _____

Since models must make simplifying assumptions, they obviously ignore some aspects of the real world. Although by their nature models will _____ describe all the complexities of the real world, economists strive to develop models that capture the essence of the economic process. The following question then arises: How well does a model capture the crucial elements of the process it purports to describe? We use two tests. The _____ test of the assumptions tries to judge how closely the model's simplifying assumptions conform to reality. It is often difficult if not impossible to assess this, however. Furthermore, many economists object to this approach by contending that simplifying assumptions are necessarily unrealistic. They advocate the use of the _____ method: How well does a model explain and predict real-world events?

POSITIVE VERSUS NORMATIVE ECONOMICS

22. _____

23. _____

_____ economics analyzes how and why resources are actually allocated in the economy. _____ analysis studies whether or not resources are allocated correctly.

MULTIPLE-CHOICE QUESTIONS

24. _____ Scarcity exists because
    a. the price of goods is too low.
    b. the price of goods is too high.
    c. there are not enough productive resources to satisfy all human wants.
    d. corporations seek to maximize profits.
    e. a and c.

25. _____ Economists study how
    a. scarce resources are allocated among alternative end uses.
    b. decisions to use land, labor, and capital in productive processes are made.
    c. firms make decisions.
    d. none of the above.
    e. a, b, and c.

26. _____ Productive processes do not include the
   a. growing of wheat.
   b. weaving of cloth.
   c. eating of food.
   d. production of missiles.
   e. a, b, and d.

27. _____ Scarcity exists in
   a. less developed nations.
   b. socialist nations.
   c. capitalist nations.
   d. industrialized nations.
   e. all of the above.

28. _____ In formulating models, economists
   a. make simplifying assumptions.
   b. capture all the complexities of the real world.
   c. prove how lazy they are.
   d. ignore no aspects of the real world.
   e. a and c.

29. _____ Direct tests to verify a model involve
   a. seeing how well the model explains and predicts real-world events.
   b. performing laboratory experiments.
   c. seeing how closely the model's assumptions conform to reality.
   d. replicating previously performed experiments.
   e. all of the above.

30. _____ Indirect tests to verify a model involve
   a. seeing how well the model explains and predicts real-world events.
   b. performing laboratory experiments.
   c. seeing how closely the model's assumptions conform to reality.
   d. replicating previously performed experiments.
   e. a and b.

31. _____ Positive economics
    a. studies how resources should be allocated.
    b. studies only those aspects of economics about which all economists agree.
    c. studies only those aspects of economics about which all economists disagree.
    d. describes how and why resources are allocated.
    e. a and c.

32. _____ Normative economics
    a. studies how resources should be allocated.
    b. studies only those aspects of economics about which all economists agree.
    c. studies only those aspects of economics about which all economists disagree.
    d. describes how and why resources are allocated.
    e. a and c.

RUNNING GLOSSARY

33. _____ _____: the study of the economic choices individuals and firms make.

34. _____ Models: simple theoretical descriptions that capture the _____ of how the economy works.

35. _____ Supply-demand model: a model describing how a good's price is determined by the behavior of the _____ who buy the good and the firms that sell it.

36. _____ Law of _____ returns: hypothesis that the cost associated with producing one more unit of a good rises as more of that good is produced.

37. _____ Equilibrium price: the price at which both buyers and sellers are in agreement about the _____ of the good being sold.

38. _____ Partial equilibrium model: an economic model of a _____ market.

39. _____ _____ equilibrium model: an economic model of a complete system of markets.

Production possibility frontier: a graph showing all possible
40. _____ _____ of goods that can be produced with a fixed amount of resources.

41. _____ _____ cost: the amount of one good that cannot be produced if more of another good is produced.

Direct approach: verifies an economic model by examining
42. _____ the validity of the _____ on which the model is based.

43. _____ _____ approach: verifies an economic model by examining how accurately it predicts and explains real-world events.

44. _____ _____ economic analysis: theories that explain how resources actually are used in an economy.

ANSWERS

1. Scarcity	16. partial	31. d
2. Economics	17. general	32. a
3. Microeconomics	18. downward	33. Microeconomics
4. simplifying	19. never	34. essence
5. most	20. direct	35. individuals
6. diminishing	21. indirect	36. diminishing
7. increases	22. Positive	37. quantity
8. consumption	23. Normative	38. single
9. last	24. c	39. General
10. next	25. e	40. combinations
11. decreases	26. c	41. Opportunity
12. downward	27. e	42. assumptions
13. increases	28. a	43. Indirect
14. upward	29. c	44. Positive
15. equilibrium	30. a	

APPENDIX TO CHAPTER 1

MATHEMATICS USED IN MICROECONOMICS

LEARNING OBJECTIVES
- The graph of a linear function is a straight line.
- The graph of a nonlinear function is curved.
- A contour line illustrates all the combinations of the independent variables that keep the dependent variable at a constant value.

WALKING TOUR SUMMARIES

FUNCTIONS OF ONE VARIABLE: Y = f(X)

1. _____ Y is a *function* of X. The value of Y depends on the value of X. Y is the _____ variable, X is the independent variable.

GRAPHING FUNCTIONS OF ONE VARIABLE

Linear Functions

2. _____ The graph of a *linear function* is a(n) _____ line.
3. _____ The *Y-intercept* is the value Y takes on when X is _____ .
4. _____ The *X-intercept* is the value X takes on when _____ is zero. The slope is the ratio of the change in Y to the
5. _____ _____ in X:

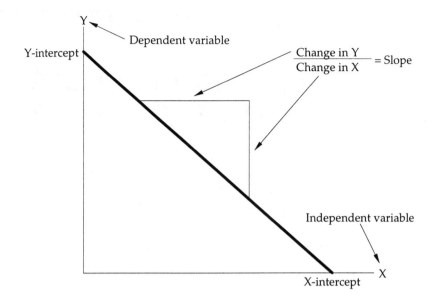

Figure 1a.1: *Linear Function*

When the Y-intercept of a linear function changes, the graph

6. _____ of the function shifts up or down in a(n) _____ fashion. When the slope changes, the graph of the function rotates

7. _____ about its _____ intercept.

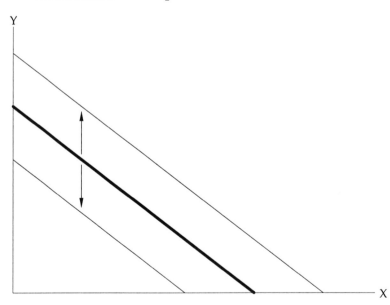

Figure 1a.2: *Changes in the Y-intercept*

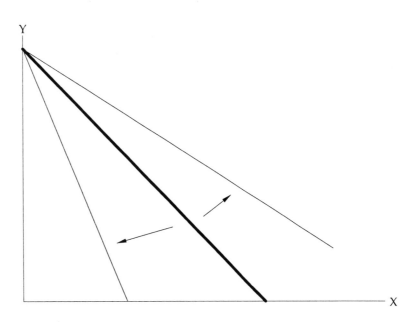

Figure 1a.3: *Changes in the Slope*

Nonlinear Functions

8. _____ The graph of a *nonlinear function* is a(n) _____ line.

The slope of a nonlinear function at a particular point is the

9. _____ slope of the straight line, which is _____ to the function at that point:

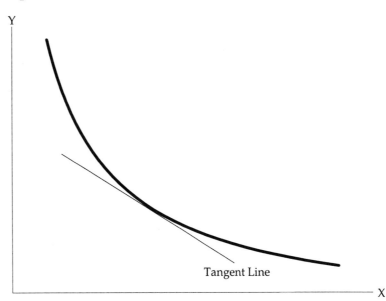

Tangent Line

Figure 1a.4: *Tangent Line for a Nonlinear Function*

10. _____ The slope of a function equals _____ whenever the function reaches its maximum or minimum value.

FUNCTIONS OF TWO VARIABLES: Y = f(X,Z)

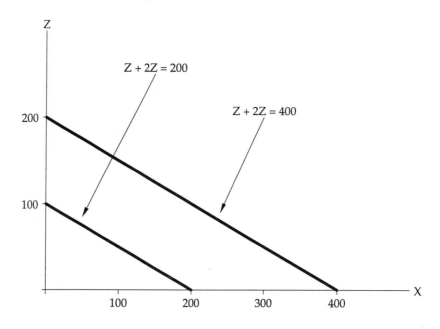

Figure 1a.5: *Contour Lines for Y = X + 2Z*

11. _____
12. _____

Y is a function of X and Z. The value of Y depends on the value of X and the value of Z. Y is the _____ variable; X and Z are the independent variables. _____ lines are used to graph functions of two or more variables. To draw a contour line first choose a constant value of Y. Then plot all the combinations of X and Z where f(X,Z) equal that constant on a graph. Repeat this procedure for several constant values of Y.

SIMULTANEOUS EQUATIONS

13. _____

The most simple example of simultaneous equations is when two variables are related by two different linear equations. The solution can be illustrated by plotting the two equations on the same graph. The point of _____ is the solution; that is, the point of intersection is the X and Y, which simultaneously meet the conditions of both equations. Figure 1a.6 illustrates the solution for the equations Y = 1.5X and Y = 200 − 0.5X:

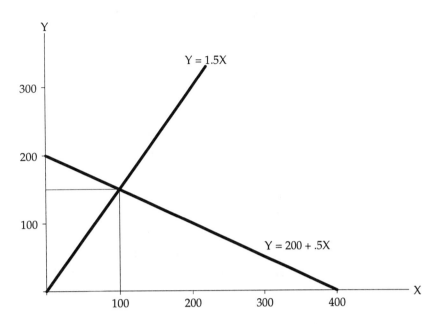

Figure 1a.6: *Simultaneous Equations*

EMPIRICAL MICROECONOMICS AND ECONOMETRICS

14. _____

15. _____

16. _____

Econometrics assesses the validity of a model by comparing the model's predictions with _____-world data. Two issues always arise in making this assessment. First, economic models can never be expected to predict with perfect accuracy as a consequence of _____ events. Econometric techniques attempt to filter out the random events so that the basic underlying relationship can emerge. Second, economists often employ the *ceteris* _____ assumption, which assumes that all other things are held constant. In the real world, many things change at the same time, however. Consequently, econometrics must account for the effect that these changes have.

MULTIPLE-CHOICE QUESTIONS

17. _____ If Y is a function of X then the
   - a. values of X and Y are unrelated.
   - b. values of X and Y are determined simultaneously.
   - c. value of Y is determined by the value of X.
   - d. value of X is determined by the value of Y.
   - e. sum of X and Y is constant.

18. _____ If Y is a function of X then
   - a. Y is called the dependent variable.
   - b. X is called the dependent variable.
   - c. Y is called the independent variable.
   - d. X is called the independent variable.
   - e. a and d.

19. _____ The graph of a linear function must be
   - a. upward sloping.
   - b. downward sloping.
   - c. straight.
   - d. curved.
   - e. none of the above.

20. _____ The X-intercept of a linear function is
   - a. the value X equals when Y equals 0.
   - b. the value Y equals when X equals 0.
   - c. where the function's graph intersects the X-axis.
   - d. where the function's graph intersects the Y-axis.
   - e. a and c.

21. _____ The Y-intercept of a linear function is
   - a. the value X equals when Y equals 0.
   - b. the value Y equals when X equals 0.
   - c. where the function's graph intersects the X-axis.
   - d. where the function's graph intersects the 45° degree line.
   - e. b and d.

22. _____ The slope of a linear function equals
   - a. the X-intercept divided by the Y-intercept.
   - b. the Y-intercept divided by the X-intercept.
   - c. the change in X divided by the change in Y.
   - d. the change in Y divided by the change in X.
   - e. a and c.

23. _____ When the Y-intercept of a linear function changes with no change in slope, the graph must
    a. shift in a parallel fashion.
    b. rotate about the X-intercept.
    c. rotate about the Y-intercept.
    d. shift toward the origin.
    e. a and d.

24. _____ When the slope of a linear function changes with no change in the Y-intercept, the graph must
    a. shift in a parallel fashion.
    b. rotate about the X-intercept.
    c. rotate about the Y-intercept.
    d. shift toward the origin.
    e. a and b.

25. _____ When Y is a function of X, the marginal effect
    a. refers to the change in X that has little or no effect on Y.
    b. refers to the change in Y resulting from a small change in X.
    c. equals the ratio of Y to X.
    d. equals the slope of the function.
    e. b and d.

26. _____ When Y is a function of X, the average effect
    a. refers to the change in X that has little or no effect on Y.
    b. refers to the change in Y resulting from a small change in X.
    c. equals the ratio of Y to X.
    d. equals the slope of the function.
    e. b and d.

27. _____ If Y is a function of X and Z then
    a. the value of Y is determined by the values of X and Z.
    b. X and Z are the dependent variables.
    c. Y is the dependent variable.
    d. X and Z are the independent variables.
    e. a, c, and d.

28. _____ Contour lines are
    a. always straight lines.
    b. always curved lines.
    c. always upward sloping.
    d. always downward sloping.
    e. used to graph functions of two or more variables.

29. _____ The points that lie on the same contour line must keep the value of
the function
   a. equal to zero.
   b. constant.
   c. positive.
   d. negative.
   e. equal to or greater than zero.

30. _____ Graphically the solution to a system of two equations is depicted
by
   a. the midpoint of their X-intercepts.
   b. the midpoint of their Y-intercepts.
   c. the intersection of the two equations.
   d. none of the above.
   e. a and b.

RUNNING GLOSSARY

31. _____ _____: the basic elements of algebra, usually called
X, Y, etc., that may be given any numerical value in an
equation.

32. _____ Functional notation: a way of denoting the fact that the
value of one variable (Y) _____ on the value of
another variable (X) or a set of variables.

33. _____ Independent variable: a variable that is _____ by the
action of other variables and may be assigned any value.

34. _____ _____ variable: a variable whose value is determined
by another variable or set of variables.

35. _____ Linear function: an equation that is represented by a
_____ line graph.

36. _____ Y-intercept: the value of Y when X equals _____.

37. _____ X-intercept: the value of _____ when Y equals zero.

38. _____ _____ effect: the change in Y resulting from a one
unit change in X.

39. _____ Simultaneous equations: a set of equations with more than one variable that must be solved _____ for a particular solution.

40. _____ Contour lines: lines in two dimensions that show the sets of values of the independent variables that yield the _____ value for the dependent variable.

41. _____ _____: the field of economics that assesses the validity of economic models.

ANSWERS

1. dependent	15. random	29. b
2. straight	16. *paribus*	30. c
3. zero	17. c	31. Variables
4. Y	18. e	32. depends
5. change	19. c	33. unaffected
6. parallel	20. e	34. Dependent
7. Y	21. b	35. straight
8. curved	22. d	36. zero
9. tangent	23. a	37. X
10. zero	24. c	38. Marginal
11. dependent	25. e	39. together
12. Contour	26. c	40. same
13. intersection	27. e	41. Econometrics
14. real	28. e	

PART 1

INTRODUCTION

WALKING TOUR PROBLEMS

LINEAR EQUATION REVIEW

1. Consider the equation: $Y = 6 - 3X$

    a. Graph the line.

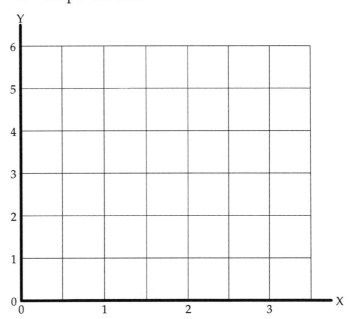

    b. What is the X-intercept?

1. _____

2. _____

The line described by the above equation crosses the X-axis at its X-intercept. Since Y is _____ all along the X-axis, the X-intercept is what X equals whenever _____ is 0.

$$0 = 6 - 3X$$
$$3X = 6$$
$$X = 2$$

The answer is 2.

c. What is the Y-intercept?

3. _____

4. _____

The line described by the above equation crosses the Y-axis at its Y-intercept. Since _____ is 0 all along the Y-axis, the Y-intercept is what _____ equals whenever X is 0.

$$Y = 6 - 2(0)$$
$$Y = 6$$

The answer is 6.0.

d. What is the slope?

5. _____

6. _____

7. _____

8. _____

9. _____

10. _____

The _____ of a straight line is the ratio of the change in Y to the change in X as one moves between any two points on the line. To calculate the slope, first choose two points lying on the line. Then determine how much Y changes between the two points and how much X changes. Last, _____ the change in Y by the change in X. We have already found two points on the line, the two intercepts. The X-intercept is _____; hence, the point (2,0) is on the line. The Y-intercept is 6; hence, the point (_____) is on the line also. Moving from the X-intercept to the Y-intercept, X decreases by _____ (from 2 to 0) and Y increases by _____ (from 0 to 6). The slope is (6/−2) = −3.

The answer is −3.

2. Consider the equation: $8X + 4Y = 32$

   a. Graph the line.

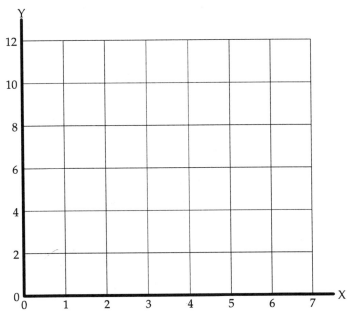

   b. What is the X-intercept?

11. _____

12. _____

13. _____

The line described by the above equation crosses the _____-axis at its X-intercept. Y is zero all along the _____-axis; the X-intercept is what X equals whenever Y is _____.

$$8X + 4(0) = 32$$
$$8X = 32$$
$$X = 4$$

The answer is 4.

   c. What is the Y-intercept?

14. _____

15. _____

16. _____

The line described by the above equation crosses the Y axis at the _____-intercept. X equals zero all along the _____-axis; the Y-intercept is what Y equals whenever _____ is zero.

$$8(0) + 4Y = 32$$
$$4Y = 32$$
$$Y = 8$$

The answer is 8.

d. What is the slope?

17. _____

The slope of a straight line is the _____ of the change in Y to the change in X as one moves between any two points on the line. To calculate the slope first choose two points lying on the line. Then determine how much Y changes between the two points and how much X changes. Last, divide the change in Y by the change in X. We have already found two points on the line, the two intercepts. The X-intercept is 4;

18. _____
19. _____

hence, the point (_____) is on the line. The Y-intercept is _____; hence, the point (0,8) is on the line also. Moving from the X-intercept to the Y-

20. _____

intercept, X decreases by _____ (from 4 to 0) and Y increases by 8 (from 0 to 8). The slope is $(8/{-}4) = -2$.

The answer is -2.

3. The equation is $4X + 12Y = -36$

21. _____ a. What is the X-intercept?

22. _____ b. What is the Y-intercept?

23. _____ c. What is the slope?

4. The equation is $20X - 5Y = 100$

24. _____ a. What is the X-intercept?

25. _____ b. What is the Y-intercept?

26. _____ c. What is the slope?

5. The equation is $Y = 25 - 5X$

27. _____ a. What is the X-intercept?

28. _____ b. What is the Y-intercept?

29. _____ c. What is the slope?

CONTOUR LINE REVIEW

1. Consider the contour line XZ = 20 and the point X = 5 and Z = 3.

    a. Graph the contour line.

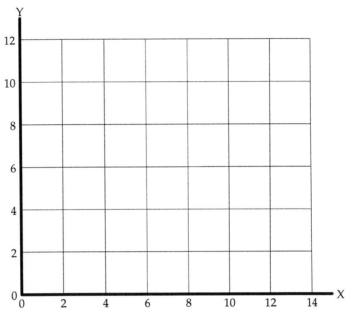

    b. Is the point below, above, or on the contour line?

At the point X = 5 and Z = 3, the function XZ = (5)(3)

30. _____   = _____. Since 15 is less than 20, the point is

31. _____   _____ the contour line.

The answer is below.

2. Consider the contour line XZ = 100 and the point X = 20 and Z = 6.

   a. Graph the contour line.

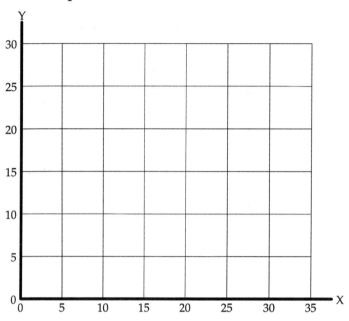

   b. Is the point below, above, or on the contour line?

32. _____ At the point X = 20 and Z = 6, the function XZ = (20)(6) = 120. Since 120 is greater than _____, the point is above the contour line.

   The answer is above.

3. Consider the contour line XZ = 160 and the point X = 4 and Z = 40. Is the point below, above, or on the contour

33. _____ line?

4. Consider the contour line XZ = 10 and the point X = 3

34. _____ and Z = 4. Is the point below, above, or on the contour line?

5. Consider the contour line XZ = 50 and the point X = 3

35. _____ and Z = 20. Is the point below, above, or on the contour line?

ANSWERS

1. 0	13. 0	25. −20
2. Y	14. Y	26. 4
3. X	15. Y	27. 5
4. Y	16. X	28. 25
5. slope	17. ratio	29. −5
6. divide	18. 4,0	30. 15
7. 2	19. 8	31. below
8. 0,6	20. 4	32. 100
9. 2	21. −9	33. on
10. 6	22. −3	34. above
11. X	23. −1/3	35. above
12. X	24. 5	

PART 2

DEMAND

CHAPTER 2

UTILITY AND CHOICE

LEARNING OBJECTIVES
- Utility measures how satisfied a particular individual is.
- Marginal rate of substitution represents how an individual can substitute goods while remaining just as well off.
- Indifference curves illustrate all the combinations of goods that keep an individual just as well off.
- Budget constraints illustrate all the combinations of goods that an individual can afford.
- Each individual seeks to maximize his/her utility subject to his/her budget constraint.

WALKING TOUR SUMMARIES

UTILITY

Economists define *utility* as the satisfaction an individual receives from the various activities he/she pursues. We shall focus our attention on two particular activities: the consumption of good X and the consumption of good Y. We represent the utility of an individual by the following function:

   Utility = U(X, Y; other things).

The utility an individual receives depends on the quantity of good X consumed, the quantity of good Y consumed, and

1. _____ "other things." By using the _____ *paribus* assumption that "other things" do not change, we can simplify the utility function:

   Utility = U(X, Y).

2. _____

Economists use an individual's utility function to describe how the individual ranks various _____ of goods. In our case, a bundle of goods consists of a specific amount of good X and a specific amount of good Y. If the individual prefers a particular bundle of goods, bundle A, to a second bundle of goods, bundle B, then the utility he/she derives

3. _____

from A will _____ the utility derived from B. If the individual finds bundles A and B equally attractive, then the

4. _____

utility of A will _____ the utility of B. Last, if he/she prefers bundle B to bundle A, the utility of B will

5. _____

_____ the utility of A.

ASSUMPTIONS ABOUT UTILITY

Consistency of Preferences
When considering any two bundles A and B, we assume that an individual will either prefer A to B, or prefer B to A, or will find them equally attractive. If this condition is met, we say that preferences are *complete*. Second, we assume that preferences are *transitive*. Consider three bundles A, B, and C. If an individual prefers A to B and

6. _____

also prefers B to C, then he/she _____ A to C.

More Is Better
An individual always prefers to consume more of a good.

INDIFFERENCE CURVES

7. _____

To construct a(n) _____ *curve* for an individual first choose a particular level of utility. The indifference curve illustrates all the different bundles that will provide the individual with the specified level of utility. That is, an indifference curve illustrates all the combinations of good X and good Y that will provide the individual with a particular level of utility. An indifference curve is a

8. _____

_____ line of the utility function. Whenever two

9. _____

bundles lie on the _____ indifference curve, the individual finds them equally attractive. The individual prefers a bundle on the indifference curve to any bundle

10. _____

lying _____ the curve. He/she prefers any bundle

11. _____

lying above to a bundle _____ the indifference curve.

MARGINAL RATE OF SUBSTITUTION (MRS)

12. _____ An individual's *marginal rate of* _____ of good X for Y equals the amount of good Y the individual is willing to give up in order to get one additional unit of good X; it represents the ratio by which the individual is willing to substitute the goods. An individual's marginal rate of substitution depends on the bundle of goods he/she is now consuming. As the individual consumer substitutes more and more X for Y, his/her marginal rate of substitution

13. _____ _____. We call this phenomenon *diminishing marginal rate of substitution*.

INDIFFERENCE CURVES AND THE MARGINAL RATE OF SUBSTITUTION

14. _____ The _____ of an individual's indifference curve shows how the individual can substitute the goods while remaining at the same level of utility. This slope equals the ratio by which the individual is willing to substitute good X for good Y, his/her marginal rate of substitution. The slope of an individual's indifference curve and his/her marginal rate of substitution represent the same thing.

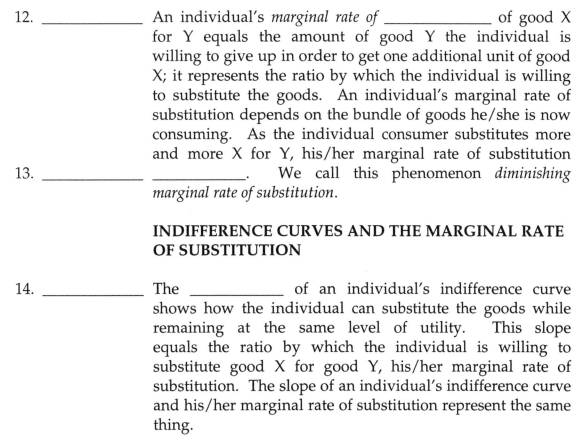

Figure 2.1: *Indifference Curve*

THE BUDGET CONSTRAINT

An individual's *budget constraint* illustrates all the bundles that the individual can afford with his/her fixed amount of _____. That is, an individual's budget constraint illustrates all the combinations of good X and good Y that the individual can afford. An individual cannot afford bundles that lie _____ his/her budget constraint. The _____-intercept of the budget constraint represents how much of good Y the individual could buy if he/she spent all his/her income on good Y. The Y-intercept just equals his/her income divided by the price of good Y, I/P_Y. Similarly, the _____-intercept equals I/P_X. The slope of the budget constraint is the _____ of the price ratio, $-(P_X/P_Y)$.

15. _____

16. _____

17. _____

18. _____

19. _____

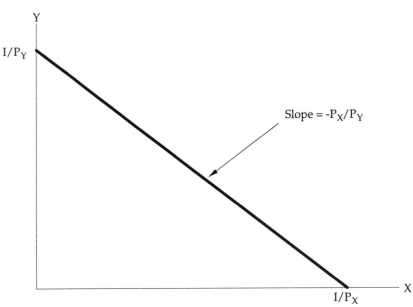

Figure 2.2: *Budget Constraint*

UTILITY MAXIMIZATION

Of all the bundles of goods an individual can afford, he/she will choose that bundle which provides him/her with the _____ utility. On the graph, the individual will choose that bundle on his/her budget constraint that maximizes his/her utility. The individual's indifference curve passing through the utility maximizing bundle will be _____ to the budget constraint. In this situation, any bundle that the individual prefers will lie _____ his/her budget constraint; he/she cannot afford to purchase

20. _____

21. _____

22. _____

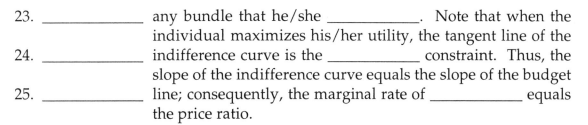

23. _____ any bundle that he/she _____. Note that when the individual maximizes his/her utility, the tangent line of the

24. _____ indifference curve is the _____ constraint. Thus, the slope of the indifference curve equals the slope of the budget

25. _____ line; consequently, the marginal rate of _____ equals the price ratio.

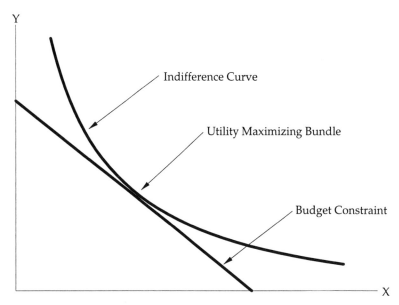

Figure 2.3: *Utility Maximization*

MULTIPLE-CHOICE QUESTIONS

26. _____ An individual's utility
    a. depends on the quantities of goods he/she consumes.
    b. refers to how valuable he/she is to society.
    c. is defined to be the satisfaction that he/she receives from the various activities he/she pursues.
    d. refers to how adaptable his job skills are.
    e. a and c.

27. _____ To economists a bundle of goods consists of
    a. all goods that can be bundled, that is, all goods that can be transported.
    b. the goods that individuals purchase at a supermarket.
    c. only goods that are perishable.
    d. specific amounts of all goods that individuals consume.
    e. a and b.

28. _____ Economists use utility functions to
   a. measure how much income an individual earns.
   b. describe how an individual ranks various bundles of goods.
   c. describe how firms decide upon the level of production.
   d. describe how firms decide upon the inputs to use.
   e. c and d.

29. _____ When comparing bundles A and B, an individual with consistent preferences will prefer
   a. A to B only if he/she has transitive preferences.
   b. A to B only if he/she can afford to buy A.
   c. A to B only if he/she can afford to buy A, but cannot afford to buy B.
   d. A to B, prefer B to A, or find A and B equally attractive.
   e. B to A only if both can be afforded.

30. _____ If an individual who has transitive preferences prefers bundle A to B and prefers bundle B to C, then he/she prefers A to C
   a. only if preferences are consistent.
   b. only if A contains more of every good.
   c. only if he/she can afford to purchase A.
   d. only if he/she can afford to purchase both.
   e. always.

31. _____ An individual's indifference curve
   a. is downward sloping.
   b. is upward sloping.
   c. is a contour line of the utility function.
   d. illustrates all the bundles an individual can afford to purchase.
   e. a and c.

32. _____ If bundle A lies on an individual's indifference curve and bundle B lies on the same curve the individual
   a. prefers A to B, if he/she can afford A.
   b. prefers B to A, if he/she can afford B.
   c. always finds A and B equally attractive.
   d. always prefers A to B.
   e. always prefers B to A.

33. _____ If bundle A lies on an individual's indifference curve and bundle B lies above the curve, the individual
    a. prefers A to B, if he/she can afford A.
    b. prefers B to A, if he/she can afford B.
    c. always finds A and B equally attractive.
    d. always prefers A to B.
    e. always prefers B to A.

34. _____ If bundle A lies on an individual's indifference curve and bundle B lies below the curve, the individual
    a. prefers A to B, if he/she can afford A.
    b. prefers B to A, if he/she can afford B.
    c. always finds A and B equally attractive.
    d. always prefers A to B.
    e. always prefers B to A.

35. _____ An individual's marginal rate of substitution of X for Y
    a. represents the ratio by which the individual is willing to substitute good X for good Y.
    b. depends on the bundle presently consumed.
    c. represents the ratio by which the individual can trade goods in the marketplace.
    d. always equals the price ratio.
    e. a and b.

36. _____ Graphically, the marginal rate of substitution is indicated by the slope of the
    a. line connecting the origin to the point on the individual's indifference curve that represents the bundle being consumed.
    b. indifference curve at the point representing the bundle being consumed.
    c. line connecting the origin to the point on the individual's utility function that represents the bundle being consumed.
    d. utility function at the point representing the bundle being consumed.
    e. b and d.

37. _____ As an individual substitutes more and more X for Y, his marginal rate of substitution of X for Y
     a. typically increases.
     b. typically decreases.
     c. typically remains the same.
     d. may increase or remain constant, but cannot decrease.
     e. must increase.

38. _____ An individual's budget constraint
     a. is upward sloping.
     b. is a contour line of the utility function.
     c. illustrates all the bundles the individual can afford to purchase.
     d. a and b.
     e. a and c.

39. _____ The slope of an individual's budget constraint
     a. is the negative of the price ratio.
     b. represents the ratio by which the individual can trade goods in the marketplace.
     c. represents the ratio by which the individual is willing to substitute good X for good Y.
     d. a and b.
     e. a and c.

40. _____ The Y-intercept of an individual's budget constraint equals
     a. his/her income divided by the price of Y.
     b. his/her income divided by the price of X.
     c. how much Y the individual can purchase if he/she buys no X and spends all his income on good Y.
     d. how much X the individual can purchase if he/she spends half his/her income on good X.
     e. a and c.

41. _____ When an individual maximizes his utility, he/she consumes a bundle of goods that lies
     a. above the budget constraint.
     b. below the budget constraint.
     c. on the budget constraint.
     d. above his utility curve.
     e. none of the above.

42. _____ When an individual maximizes his/her utility,
   a. the indifference curve passing through his bundle must be tangent to the budget line.
   b. his marginal rate of substitution equals the price ratio.
   c. his marginal rate of substitution must equal the slope of the utility function.
   d. all bundles that he/she prefers must lie above the budget line.
   e. a, b, and d.

RUNNING GLOSSARY

43. _____ Theory of choice: the interaction of preferences and _____ that causes people to make the choices they do.

44. _____ _____: the pleasure, satisfaction, or need fulfillment that people get from their economic activity.

45. _____ Ceteris paribus assumption: in economic analysis, holding all _____ factors constant so that only the factor being studied is allowed to change.

46. _____ _____ preferences: the assumption that an individual is able to state which of any two possible options is preferred.

47. _____ Transitivity of preferences: the property that if A is preferred to B, and B is preferred to C, then A must be _____ to C.

48. _____ Marginal rate of _____ (MRS): the rate at which an individual is willing to trade one good for another while remaining equally well-off.

49. _____ _____ curve: all the combinations of goods or services that provide the same level of utility.

50. _____ Indifference curve map: a(n) _____ map that shows the utility an individual obtains from all possible consumption options.

51. _____ _____ constraint: the limit that income places on the combinations of goods and services that an individual can buy.

Composite good: treating expenditures on several different goods whose relative prices do not change as a(n)

52. _____ _____good for convenience in analysis.

ANSWERS

1. *ceteris*	19. negative	37. b
2. bundles	20. most	38. c
3. exceed	21. tangent	39. d
4. equal	22. above	40. e
5. exceed	23. prefers	41. c
6. prefers	24. budget	42. e
7. indifference	25. substitution	43. income
8. contour	26. c	44. Utility
9. same	27. d	45. other
10. below	28. b	46. Complete
11. on	29. d	47. preferred
12. substitution	30. e	48. substitution
13. decreases	31. e	49. Indifference
14. slope	32. c	50. contour
15. income	33. e	51. Budget
16. above	34. d	52. single
17. Y	35. e	
18. X	36. b	

CHAPTER 3

INDIVIDUALS' DEMANDS

LEARNING OBJECTIVES

- A demand function relates the quantity demanded to prices, income, and preferences.
- An income effect occurs whenever real purchasing power changes.
- More (less) of a normal (inferior) good is purchased when income increases.
- A substitution effect occurs whenever the ratio of prices changes.
- When the price of a good changes, both a substitution and income effect ensue.
- If two goods are substitutes and the price of one good increases, the quantity demanded of the other good increases.
- If two goods are complements and the price of one good increases, the quantity demanded of the other good decreases.
- An ordinary demand curve indicates how the quantity demanded changes when the price of the good changes while all other prices and income remain constant.
- A compensated demand curve indicates how the quantity demanded changes when the price of the good changes while all other prices and utility remain constant.
- Consumer surplus represents the value consumers receive from the consumption of a good in excess of what they pay for it.

WALKING TOUR SUMMARIES

DEMAND FUNCTIONS

1. _____

2. _____

We have argued that the bundle of goods an individual chooses depends upon his/her _____ constraint and his/her preferences. The quantities of good X and Y demanded depend upon the budget constraint and preferences. An individual's _____ and the prices of X and Y determine his/her budget constraint. Therefore, we can represent his/her *demand function* with the following equation:

Quantity of X Demanded = $X = d_X(P_X, P_Y, I;$ preferences$)$.

HOMOGENEITY: WHAT HAPPENS WHEN ALL PRICES AND INCOME CHANGE BY THE SAME PERCENTAGE?

If all prices and income change by the same percentage, the quantities of X and Y demanded are

3. _____ _____. To understand why, note that when all prices and income change by the same percentage, the budget

4. _____ constraint is _____. Thus, the individual will still choose the same bundle of goods.

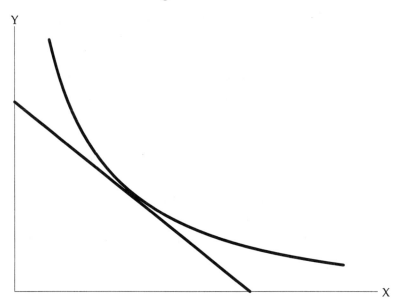

Figure 3.1: *All Prices Change by the Same Percentage*

CHANGE IN INCOME: WHAT HAPPENS WHEN INCOME ALONE CHANGES?

Whenever an individual's income rises and prices do not change, his/her budget constraint shifts out, away from the

5. _____ origin. Since the _____ of the budget depends only on the ratio of prices, the slope does not change; thus,

6. _____ the budget line shifts in a(n) _____ fashion. Such a

7. _____ shift causes a(n) _____ effect. The income effect represents a change in real purchasing power; the individual can now afford bundles that contain more of both goods. The quantity of X that the individual demands after his/her income rises may increase, decrease, or remain the

8. _____ same. Economists refer to a good as _____ whenever the quantity X demanded increases with a rise in income. Alternatively, if an increase in income causes the quantity

- 40 -

9. _____ demanded to decrease, we call the good _____. An
10. _____ _____ Curve illustrates the relationship between the quantity of X demanded and income.

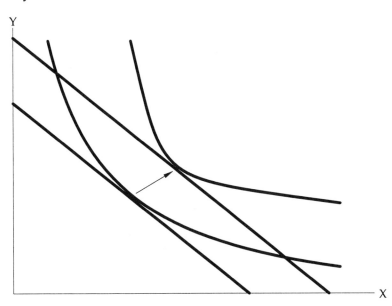

Figure 3.2: *Income Alone Changes*

CHANGE IN A GOOD'S PRICE: WHAT HAPPENS WHEN THE PRICE OF GOOD X ALONE CHANGES?

Whenever the price of good X falls, the budget constraint
11. _____ shifts out, but not in a(n) _____ fashion. It rotates
12. _____ about the _____-intercept becoming less steep. To understand why, recall that the Y-intercept depicts the situation in which the individual spends all
13. _____ his/her income on good _____. Since neither income nor the price of good Y has changed, the Y-intercept remains unchanged. The X-intercept (which depicts the situation in which the individual spends all his/her income on good X)
14. _____ _____, however, because the price of good X has fallen.

Two effects now come into play. The change in the slope of the budget constraint reflects the fact that good X
15. _____ has become _____ expensive relative to good Y. Therefore, we would expect the individual to substitute good X for good Y. If the individual were to stay on the same indifference curve, he/she would now substitute X for Y. He/she would equate his/her marginal rate of
16. _____ _____ to the new price ratio. As a result of this

- 41 -

17. _____ _____effect, the individual will consume more of good X and less of good Y. Second, recall that the budget constraint has shifted out. The fall in the price of X without any change in income has increased the individual's real

18. _____ purchasing power. There is a(n) _____ effect, also. The individual can now afford bundles that contain more of both goods. As a result of the income effect, the individual would consume more good X, if good X is a

19. _____ _____ good. He/she would consume less X, if X is

20. _____ _____.

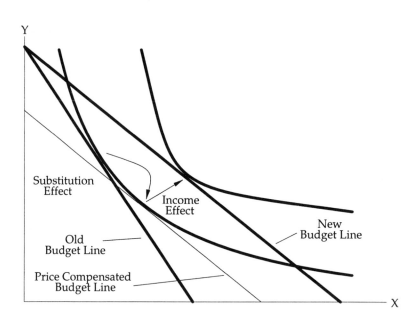

Figure 3.3: *Decrease in the Price of Good X*

TOTAL EFFECT ON THE QUANTITY OF GOOD X DEMANDED WHEN THE PRICE OF GOOD X CHANGES

21. _____ Whenever good X is _____, the substitution and income effects work together; a fall in the price of good X

22. _____ will unambiguously lead to a(n) _____ quantity of X demanded. On the other hand, whenever good X is

23. _____ _____, the substitution and income effects work against each other. If the price of the good falls, the

24. _____ substitution effect leads to a(n) _____ in the quantity

25. _____ of X while the income effect leads to a(n) _____.

26. _____ With a(n) _____ good the net result depends upon which of the two effects is stronger. A fall in the price

27. _____

28. _____

decreases the quantity demanded whenever the _____ effect dominates. Economists refer to such cases as _____ Paradox.

SUBSTITUTES AND COMPLEMENTS

29. _____

30. _____

Good X is a (gross) *substitute* for good Y if an increase in the price of good Y _____ the quantity of good X demanded. Good X is a (gross) _____ of good Y if an increase in the price of good Y decreases the quantity of good X demanded.

INDIVIDUAL DEMAND CURVE

31. _____

32. _____

33. _____

34. _____

35. _____

36. _____

37. _____

38. _____

39. _____

An *individual's demand curve* for good X illustrates the relationship between the quantity of good X demanded by the individual and the price of good X. Along a single demand curve, all factors that affect demand besides the price of the good itself do not change. The demand curve for good X will be downward sloping unless the good is a _____ good. The demand curve can shift only when a factor relevant to the demand for good X other than the _____ of good X itself changes. When this happens a change in _____ occurs. If the demand curve shifts to the right, there is a(n) _____ in demand. If it shifts to the left, there is a(n) _____ in demand. A change in the price of good X itself never causes the demand curve to _____, but rather leads to a movement _____ the demand curve. Economists refer to a movement along a demand curve as a change in the _____ demanded. An increase in the price of X _____ the quantity of good X demanded unless the good is a Giffen good. Alternatively, a decrease in the price increases the quantity demanded.

- 43 -

ORDINARY AND COMPENSATED DEMAND CURVES

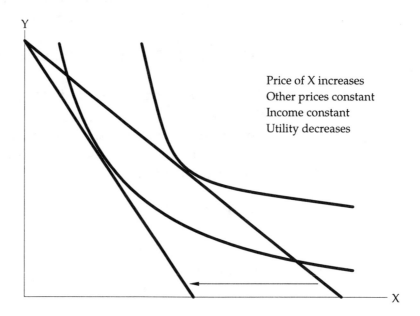

Figure 3.4: *Derivation of an Ordinary Demand Curve*

An ordinary demand curve illustrates how the quantity demanded of a good changes when the good's price changes, while keeping all other prices and

40. _____ _____ unchanged. As one moves on a standard demand curve, utility changes. For example, when the price of good X increases, the budget constraint rotates inward,

41. _____ making the consumer _____ off.   When moving along an ordinary demand curve, the price of the good itself

42. _____ and utility _____, all other prices and income remain constant.   An ordinary demand curve reflects both a

43. _____ substitution and _____ effect.

44. _____ A(n) _____ demand curve illustrates how the quantity demanded of a good changes when the good's price changes, while keeping all other prices and utility unchanged. As one moves along a compensated demand

45. _____ curve, income _____. As the good's price increases,

46. _____ the consumer needs _____ income to keep his utility constant:

- 44 -

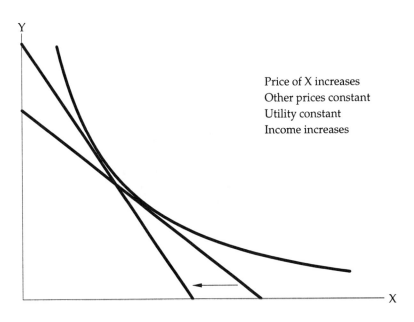

Price of X increases
Other prices constant
Utility constant
Income increases

Figure 3.5: *Derivation of a Compensated Demand Curve*

When moving along a compensated demand curve, the price of the good itself and income change, all other prices and

47. _____ _____ remain constant. The compensated demand
48. _____ implicitly provides the individual with the _____ necessary to compensate him for price changes. The compensated demand curve compensates the individual for the income effect that results from a change in the price.
49. _____ Hence, it reflects only the _____ effect.

The "triangle" beneath the compensated demand curve and above the price represents the compensation required to keep individuals just as well off, if consumption
50. _____ of the good were reduced to _____. Economists
51. _____ call this area _____ surplus. It represents the extra value individuals receive from consuming the good over what they actually pay for it. When prices change, changes in consumer surplus reflect how the _____ of
52. _____ individuals is affected.

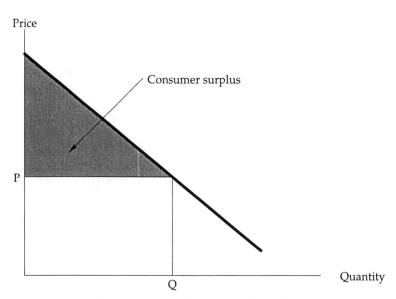

Figure 3.6: *Consumer Surplus*

MULTIPLE-CHOICE QUESTIONS

53. _____ When all prices and income increase by the same percentage, an individual's budget constraint will
    a. shift outward in a parallel fashion.
    b. shift inward in a parallel fashion.
    c. remain stationary.
    d. shift outward by rotating about the Y-intercept.
    e. shift outward by rotating about the X-intercept.

54. _____ When all prices and income increase by the same percentage, the quantity of good X demanded will
    a. increase only if X is a normal good.
    b. increase only if X is an inferior good.
    c. always remain the same.
    d. always increase.
    e. always decrease.

55. _____ When income alone increases, an individual's budget constraint will
    a. shift outward in a parallel fashion.
    b. shift inward in a parallel fashion.
    c. remain stationary.
    d. shift outward by rotating about the Y-intercept.
    e. shift outward by rotating about the X-intercept.

56. _____ When income alone increases, the quantity of X an individual demands will
   a. increase only if X is a normal good.
   b. increase only if X is an inferior good.
   c. always remain the same.
   d. always increase.
   e. always decrease.

57. _____ The Engel Curve relates quantity demanded to changes in
   a. price only.
   b. income only.
   c. price and income.
   d. utility.
   e. the marginal rate of substitution.

58. _____ If the quantity demanded increases whenever income rises, the good is called
   a. a Giffen good.
   b. a normal good.
   c. an inferior good.
   d. a necessity.
   e. b and d.

59. _____ If the quantity demanded decreases whenever income rises, the good is called
   a. a Giffen good.
   b. a normal good.
   c. an inferior good.
   d. a necessity.
   e. a and c.

60. _____ Whenever the price of good X alone decreases, the budget constraint will
   a. shift outward in a parallel fashion.
   b. shift inward in a parallel fashion.
   c. remain stationary.
   d. shift outward by rotating about the Y-intercept.
   e. shift outward by rotating about the X-intercept.

61. _____ Whenever the price of good X alone decreases, the substitution effect causes the quantity of good X to
    a. always increase.
    b. always decrease.
    c. increase only if good X is normal.
    d. increase only if good X is inferior.
    e. always remain unchanged.

62. _____ Whenever the price of good X alone decreases, the income effect causes the quantity of good X to
    a. always increase.
    b. always decrease.
    c. increase only if good X is normal.
    d. increase only if good X is inferior.
    e. always remain unchanged.

63. _____ If the good is normal and its price falls, the quantity demanded
    a. will always increase.
    b. will always decrease.
    c. will always remain the same.
    d. may increase, decrease, or remain the same.
    e. will never increase.

64. _____ If the good is inferior and its price falls, the quantity demanded
    a. will always increase.
    b. will always decrease.
    c. will always remain the same.
    d. may increase, decrease, or remain the same.
    e. will never increase.

65. _____ If the quantity demanded increases whenever the price increases, the good is called
    a. a Giffen good.
    b. a normal good.
    c. an inferior good.
    d. a necessity.
    e. b and d.

66. _____ If a good is a Giffen good, the good is
  a. normal and the income effect dominates the substitution effect.
  b. normal and the substitution effect dominates the income effect.
  c. inferior and the income effect dominates the substitution effect.
  d. inferior and the substitution effect dominates the income effect.
  e. none of the above.

67. _____ If an increase in the price of good Y leads to an increase in the quantity of good X demanded, good X is
  a. a Giffen good relative to good Y.
  b. an inferior good relative to good Y.
  c. a (gross) substitute of good Y.
  d. a (gross) complement of good Y.
  e. a normal good.

68. _____ If an increase in the price of good Y leads to a decrease in the quantity of good X demanded, good X is
  a. a Giffen good relative to good Y.
  b. an inferior good relative to good Y.
  c. a (gross) substitute of good Y.
  d. a (gross) complement of good Y.
  e. a normal good.

69. _____ An individual's demand curve for good X illustrates the quantity demanded for
  a. every price of good X holding all other factors (relevant to the demand for good X) constant.
  b. every income level holding all other factors (relevant to the demand for good X) constant.
  c. every price of good Y holding all other factors (relevant to the demand for good X) constant.
  d. every price of good X, good Y, and income level.
  e. none of the above.

70. _____ An individual's demand curve for good X shifts only when
    a. the price of good X changes.
    b. any factor relevant to the demand of good X changes.
    c. income changes.
    d. some factor relevant to the demand for good X other than the price of good X itself changes.
    e. a and c.

71. _____ If good X is not a Giffen good, an increase in the price of good X leads to
    a. an increase in demand.
    b. a decrease in demand.
    c. an increase in the quantity demanded.
    d. a decrease in the quantity demanded.
    e. b and d.

72. _____ If good X is a normal good, an increase in income leads to
    a. an increase in demand.
    b. a decrease in demand.
    c. an increase in the quantity demanded.
    d. a decrease in the quantity demanded.
    e. b and d.

73. _____ When moving along an ordinary demand curve,
    a. the prices of other goods are constant.
    b. income is constant.
    c. utility is constant.
    d. a and b.
    e. a and c.

74. _____ When moving along a compensated demand curve,
    a. the prices of other goods are constant.
    b. income is constant.
    c. utility is constant.
    d. a and b.
    e. a and c.

75. _____ Consumer surplus equals
   a. what consumers spend on the good.
   b. what consumers spend on the good plus the profits firms earn.
   c. the value consumers place on being able to consume a good in excess of what they pay for it.
   d. the area beneath the compensated demand curve.
   e. what people actually pay for the good less the compensation they would demand to voluntarily stop consuming the good.

76. _____ Consumer surplus equals
   a. the area beneath the ordinary demand curve.
   b. the area beneath the ordinary demand curve lying above the price.
   c. the area beneath the compensated demand curve.
   d. the area beneath the compensated demand curve lying above the price.
   e. none of the above.

RUNNING GLOSSARY

77. _____ _____ statics: the investigation of the new choices people make when conditions change, as compared to the choices they make under the former conditions.

78. _____ Demand function: a representation of how quantity demanded depends on _____, income, and preferences.

79. _____ Homogeneous demand function: demand does not change when prices and income increase in the same _____.

80. _____ _____ good: a good that is bought in greater quantities as income increases.

81. _____ Substitution effect: the part of the change in the quantity demanded of a good that is caused by a change in relative prices; individuals react by substituting the good that becomes relatively _____ for the other that becomes
82. _____ relatively more expensive. A movement _____ an indifference curve.

83. _____ _____ effect: the part of the change in the quantity demanded of a good that is caused by a change in real purchasing power.

84. _____ Giffen's Paradox: a situation in which the increase in a good's price leads people to consume _____ of the good.

85. _____ Complements: two goods related in such a way that when the price of one increases, the quantity demanded of the other _____.

86. _____ _____: two goods related in such a way that when the price of one increases, the quantity demanded of the other rises.

87. _____ Individual demand curve: a graphic representation of the relationship between the _____ of a good and the quantity of it demanded by a person.

88. _____ Change in _____ demanded: the increase or decrease in quantity demanded caused by a change in the good's price. Graphically represented by the movement

89. _____ _____a demand curve.

90. _____ Change in _____: the increase or decrease in demand for a good caused by changes in the price of another good, income, or preferences. Graphically represented by a

91. _____ _____ of the entire demand curve.

92. _____ Compensated demand curve: a demand curve drawn on the assumption that other prices and _____ are held constant. Income effects of price changes are compensated

93. _____ for along the curve and it reflects only _____ effects.

94. _____ _____ surplus: the extra value individuals receive from consuming a good over what they pay for it. The maximum amount people would be willing to pay for the right to consume a good at its current price.

ANSWERS

1. budget	33. demand	65. a
2. income	34. increase	66. c
3. unaffected	35. decrease	67. c
4. unchanged	36. shift	68. d
5. slope	37. along	69. a
6. parallel	38. quantity	70. d
7. income	39. decreases	71. d
8. normal	40. income	72. a
9. inferior	41. worse	73. d
10. Engel	42. change	74. e
11. parallel	43. income	75. c
12. Y	44. compensated	76. d
13. Y	45. changes	77. Comparative
14. increases	46. more	78. prices
15. less	47. utility	79. proportion
16. substitution	48. income	80. Normal
17. substitution	49. substitution	81. cheaper
18. income	50. zero	82. along
19. normal	51. consumer	83. Income
20. inferior	52. welfare	84. more
21. normal	53. c	85. falls
22. greater	54. c	86. Substitutes
23. inferior	55. a	87. price
24. increase	56. a	88. quantity
25. decrease	57. b	89. along
26. inferior	58. b	90. demand
27. income	59. c	91. shift
28. Giffen's	60. d	92. utility
29. increases	61. a	93. substitution
30. complement	62. c	94. Consumer
31. Giffen	63. a	
32. price	64. d	

CHAPTER 4

MARKET DEMAND AND ELASTICITY

LEARNING OBJECTIVES
- The market demand curve is the horizontal sum of each individual's demand curve.
- The own price elasticity of demand equals the percent change in the quantity demanded resulting from a 1 percent change in the good's own price.
- The income elasticity of demand equals the percent change in the quantity demanded resulting from a 1 percent change in income.
- The cross price elasticity of demand equals the percent change in the quantity demanded resulting from a 1 percent change in the price of another good.

WALKING TOUR SUMMARIES

MARKET DEMAND CURVES

A market demand curve illustrates the relationship between the quantity of a good demanded by all potential buyers

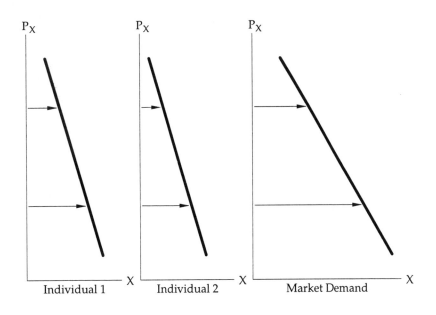

Figure 4.1: *Construction of the Market Demand Curve*

1. _____ and the _____ of the good. All factors that influence demand other than the price of the good itself are held constant. We construct a market demand curve by summing

2. _____ each individual's demand curve _____.

A market demand curve can shift only when

3. _____ something other than the _____ of the good itself changes. Economists refer to a shift of the curve as a

4. _____ _____ in demand. A change in the price of the good itself will never cause the market demand curve to shift. A change in the good's price will cause a movement

5. _____ _____ the market demand curve, however. We refer to a movement along the curve as a change in the

6. _____ _____ demanded.

ELASTICITY

Economists use the notion of elasticity to quantify the relationship between two variables. The price elasticity of demand allows us to estimate by how much the quantity demanded will change when the price of a good changes. It is important to remember that elasticities are always

7. _____ calculated in _____ terms.

PRICE ELASTICITY OF DEMAND (e_{Q,P})

The price elasticity of demand measures how sensitive the

8. _____ quantity demanded is to the _____. More specifically, the price elasticity of demand equals the percent change in quantity demanded resulting from a 1

9. _____ _____ change in the price:

$$e_{Q,P} = \frac{\text{Percent Change in Q}}{\text{Percent Change in P}}$$

Except in the case of Giffen's Paradox, the price elasticity of

10. _____ demand will be _____.

If the quantity demanded is "very" sensitive to price,

11. _____ demand is _____. More specifically, demand is elastic when a 1 percent change in price leads to a more than 1 percent change in quantity demanded. In mathematical

12. _____ terms, when $e_{Q,P}$ is _____ than −1, demand is elastic.

13. _____   On the other hand, if the quantity demanded is "not very" sensitive to price, demand is _____. More specifically, demand is inelastic when a 1 percent change in price leads to a less than 1 percent change in quantity

14. _____   demanded. When $e_{Q,P}$ is _____ than –1, demand is

15. _____   inelastic. Last, if $e_{Q,P}$ equals –1, demand is _____ elastic.

PRICE ELASTICITY AND TOTAL EXPENDITURES

Price elasticity of demand explains how the total amount consumers spend on a good, total expenditures, responds to price changes. Note that:

$$\text{Total Expenditures} = \text{Price} \times \text{Quantity.}$$

16. _____   Except for a Giffen good, quantity will _____ when the price decreases. Thus, the effect of a price change on total expenditures depends on whether a price change leads to a "large" or "small" change in the

17. _____   _____. That is, the effect depends on the price

18. _____   _____ of demand. If demand is elastic, the quantity demanded is "very" sensitive to the price. A fall in the price will lead to a "large" increase in quantity causing a(n)

19. _____   _____ in total expenditures. A rise in the price will

20. _____   cause a(n) _____ in total expenditures. On the other hand, if demand is inelastic, the quantity demanded is "not very" sensitive to the price. A fall in the price will lead to a

21. _____   "small" increase in quantity causing a(n) _____ in total expenditures. A rise in the price will cause a(n)

22. _____   _____ in total expenditures.

IS THE PRICE ELASTICITY OF DEMAND CONSTANT?

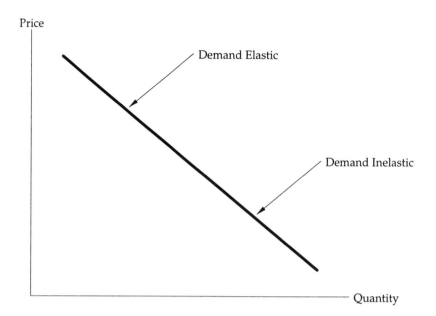

Figure 4.2: *Linear Demand Curve and Elasticity*

The price elasticity of demand need not be the same at all points on a demand curve. In fact, if the demand curve is linear (a straight line), the price elasticity of demand is different at every point. At high prices demand is

23. _____ _____; at low prices demand is inelastic. Note that the linear case illustrates that slope and elasticity are different. All points on a linear demand curve have the

24. _____ same _____, but they do not have the same elasticity.

INCOME ELASTICITY OF DEMAND

The *income elasticity of demand* measures how sensitive the quantity demanded is to a change in income. More specifically, the income elasticity of demand equals the percent change in the quantity demanded resulting from a

25. _____ 1 _____ change in income:

$$e_{Q,I} = \frac{\text{Percent Change in Q}}{\text{Percent Change in I}}$$

26. _____ The income elasticity is _____ for a normal good and
27. _____ _____ for an inferior good. Goods for which the
28. _____ income elasticity exceeds one are called _____.

- 58 -

CROSS-PRICE ELASTICITY OF DEMAND

29. _____

30. _____

The *cross-price elasticity of demand* measures how sensitive the quantity demanded of one good is to a change in the _____ _____ of another good. More specifically, the cross-price elasticity of demand equals the _____ change in the quantity demanded of one good resulting from a 1 percent change in the price of another good:

$$e_{Q,P'} = \frac{\text{Percent Change in Q}}{\text{Percent Change in P'}}$$

where P' represents the price of the other good.

EMPIRICAL STUDIES OF DEMAND

31. _____

32. _____

One serious difficulty in estimating demand elasticities concerns the *ceteris paribus* assumption. The price elasticity of demand implicitly assumes that only one determinant of demand, the _____, changes. Similarly, the income elasticity implicitly assumes that only _____ changes. In the real world, it is virtually impossible to observe a situation in which only one determinant of demand changes; many factors are changing simultaneously. Fortunately, multiple regression analysis provides economists with a statistical technique that isolates the effect of a single factor. A second difficulty arises from the fact that the price and quantity we observe reflect the intersection of the demand and supply curves. Econometric techniques must be used to identify each of the two curves.

MULTIPLE-CHOICE QUESTIONS

33. _____ A good's market demand curve indicates the quantity of the good demanded by
    a. one individual buyer.
    b. all individual buyers who historically purchase the good.
    c. all potential buyers.
    d. the average individual buyer.
    e. b and d.

34. _____ The market demand curve for good X illustrates the quantity demanded by all potential buyers for
   a. every price of good X holding all other factors (relevant to the demand for good X) constant.
   b. every income level holding all other factors (relevant to the demand for good X) constant.
   c. every price of good Y holding all other factors (relevant to the demand for good X) constant.
   d. every price of good X, good Y, and income level.
   e. a and b.

35. _____ The market demand curve for good X shifts only when
   a. the price of good X changes.
   b. any factor relevant to the demand of good X changes.
   c. income changes.
   d. some factor relevant to the demand for good X other than the price of good X changes.
   e. a and d.

36. _____ The market demand curve can be constructed by summing each individual's
   a. Engel curve horizontally.
   b. Engel curve vertically.
   c. demand curve horizontally.
   d. demand curve vertically.
   e. Engel and demand curves horizontally.

37. _____ The price elasticity of demand illustrates how sensitive the quantity demanded is to a change in
   a. its own price.
   b. income.
   c. the price of another good.
   d. utility.
   e. the marginal rate of substitution.

38. _____ The price elasticity of demand equals
    a. the change in the quantity demanded caused by a 1 unit (1 dollar) change in price.
    b. the percent change in the quantity demanded caused by a 1 percent change in price.
    c. the ratio of the change in the quantity demanded to the change in the price.
    d. the ratio of the percent change in the quantity demanded to the percent change in the price.
    e. b and d.

39. _____ If a good is a Giffen good, the elasticity of demand must be
    a. negative.
    b. positive.
    c. 1.
    d. −1.
    e. less than or equal to 0.

40. _____ If the quantity demanded is "very" sensitive to a change in the price, that is, if a 1 percent change in the price leads to a greater than 1 percent change in quantity demanded, then
    a. the price elasticity of demand is less than −1.
    b. the price elasticity of demand is greater than −1.
    c. demand is said to be unit elastic.
    d. demand is said to be inelastic.
    e. a and c.

41. _____ If the quantity demanded is "not very" sensitive to a change in the price, that is, if a 1 percent change in the price leads to a less than 1 percent change in quantity demanded, then
    a. the price elasticity of demand is less than −1.
    b. the price elasticity of demand equals −1.
    c. demand is said to be elastic.
    d. demand is said to be inelastic.
    e. demand is said to be unit elastic.

42. _____ If a 1 percent change in the price leads to a 1 percent change in quantity demanded, then
    a. the price elasticity of demand is less than −1.
    b. the price elasticity of demand is greater than −1.
    c. the price elasticity of demand equals −1.
    d. demand is said to be elastic.
    e. demand is said to be unit inelastic.

43. _____ If the price of a good whose demand is elastic falls, the total expenditures individuals make to purchase the good
    a. must increase.
    b. must decrease.
    c. must remain the same.
    d. may increase, decrease, or remain the same.
    e. may decrease or remain the same, but cannot increase.

44. _____ If the price of a good whose demand is inelastic falls, the total expenditures individuals make to purchase the good
    a. must increase.
    b. must decrease.
    c. must remain the same.
    d. may increase, decrease, or remain the same.
    e. will never decrease.

45. _____ If the price of a good whose demand is unit elastic falls, the total expenditures individuals make to purchase the good
    a. must increase.
    b. must decrease.
    c. must remain the same.
    d. may increase, decrease, or remain the same.
    e. none of the above.

46. _____ A straight line demand curve
    a. has price elasticity equal to 1 at all prices.
    b. has the same price elasticity at all prices.
    c. is elastic at low prices and inelastic at high prices.
    d. is inelastic at low prices and elastic at high prices.
    e. has a constant marginal rate of substitution.

47. _____ The income elasticity equals
    a. the change in the quantity demanded caused by a 1 unit (1 dollar) change in income.
    b. the percent change in the quantity demanded caused by a 1 percent change in income.
    c. the ratio of the change in the quantity demanded to the change in income.
    d. the ratio of the percent change in the quantity demanded to the percent change in the price.
    e. b and d.

48. _____ The income elasticity of a normal good is
  a. never positive.
  b. always positive.
  c. always negative.
  d. always zero.
  e. always one.

49. _____ The income elasticity of an inferior good is
  a. always positive.
  b. always negative.
  c. always zero.
  d. always one.
  e. never negative.

RUNNING GLOSSARY

50. _____ _____ demand: the total quantity of a good or service demanded by potential buyers.

51. _____ Market demand curve: the relationship between the total quantity demanded of a good or service and its _____, holding all other factors constant.

52. _____ Elasticity: the measure of the percent change in one variable brought about by a(n) _____ percent change in some other variable.

53. _____ _____ elasticity of demand: the percent change in the quantity demanded of a good in response to a 1 percent change in its price.

54. _____ Income elasticity of demand: the percent change in the quantity demanded of a good in response to a 1 percent change in _____.

55. _____ _____ price elasticity of demand: the percent change in the quantity demanded of a good in response to a 1 percent change in the price of another good.

ANSWERS

1. price
2. horizontally
3. price
4. change
5. along
6. quantity
7. percentage
8. price
9. percent
10. negative
11. elastic
12. less
13. inelastic
14. greater
15. unit
16. increase
17. quantity
18. elasticity
19. increase

20. decrease
21. decrease
22. increase
23. elastic
24. slope
25. percent
26. positive
27. negative
28. luxuries
29. price
30. percent
31. price
32. income
33. c
34. a
35. d
36. c
37. a
38. e

39. b
40. a
41. d
42. c
43. a
44. b
45. c
46. d
47. b
48. b
49. b
50. Market
51. price
52. 1
53. Price
54. income
55. Cross-

PART 2

DEMAND

WALKING TOUR PROBLEMS

UTILITY MAXIMIZATION

1. Suppose that the price of good X is $6.00 and the price of good Y is $2.00. An individual whose income is $600.00 purchases a bundle of goods containing 60 units of good X and 120 units of good Y. The individual's marginal rate of substitution is 2.

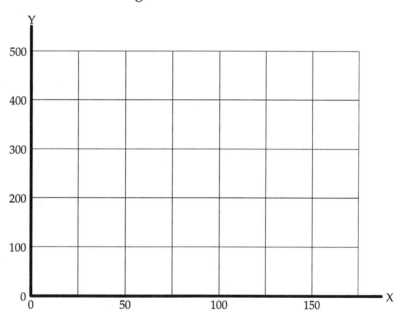

   a. Plot the budget line on the above diagram.

   b. What is the X-intercept of the individual's budget line?

   The X-intercept of the individual's budget line depicts the situation in which all income is spent on good _____. Since income is $600.00 and the price of good X is $6.00, the individual would purchase _____ units of X if all income were spent on good X.

1. _____

2. _____

The answer is 100.

c. What is the Y-intercept of the individual's budget line?

3. _____

The _____ of the individual's budget line depicts the situation in which all income is spent on good Y. Since income is $600.00 and the price of good Y is $2.00, the individual would purchase _____ units of Y if all income were spent on good Y.

4. _____

The answer is 300.

d. Does the bundle of goods purchased more than exhaust, less than exhaust, or exactly exhaust the individual's income?

The bundle contains 60 units of good X and 120 units of good Y. Since the price of good X is $6.00, $_____ is spent on good X; since the price of good Y is $2.00, $_____ is spent on good Y. A total of $_____ is spent to purchase the bundle exactly exhausting the individual's income.

5. _____
6. _____
7. _____

The answer is exactly exhaust.

e. Is the individual maximizing utility? Should more, less, or the same amount be spent on X to maximize utility?

The price ratio is ($6.00/$2.00) = 3 whereas the individual's marginal rate of substitution is 2. _____ is not being maximized because the marginal rate of substitution does not equal the price ratio.

8. _____

The answer is no.

Since the price ratio is 3, if the individual purchases 1 less unit of good X he can afford to buy 3 more units of good Y. Since the individual's marginal rate of substitution is 2, only _____ additional units

9. _____

10. _____

of good Y are required to keep him just as well off when he consumes 1 less unit of good X. Consequently, by purchasing 1 less unit of good X and 3 more units of good Y the individual becomes _____ off.

The answer is less should be spent on good X.

2. Suppose that the price of good X is $5.00 and the price of good Y is $2.00. An individual whose income is $400.00 purchases a bundle of goods containing 60 units of good X and 40 units of good Y. The individual's marginal rate of substitution is 1.25.

a. Plot the budget line on the above diagram.

b. What is the X-intercept of the individual's budget line?

11. _____

The _____ of the individual's budget line depicts the situation in which all income is spent on good X. Since income is $400.00 and the price of good X is $5.00, the individual would purchase

12. _____

_____ units of X if all income were spent on good X.

The answer is 80.

c. What is the Y-intercept of the individual's budget line?

The Y-intercept of the individual's budget line depicts the situation in which all income is spent on good _____. Since income is $400.00 and the price of good Y is $2.00, the individual would purchase _____ units of Y if all income were spent on good Y.

13. _____

14. _____

The answer is 200.

d. Does the bundle of goods purchased more than exhaust, less than exhaust, or exactly exhaust the individual's income?

The bundle contains 60 units of good X and 40 units of good Y. Since the price of good X is $5.00, $_____ is spent on good X; since the price of good Y is $2.00, $_____ is spent on good Y. A total of $380.00 is spent to purchase the bundle, _____ the individual's income.

15. _____

16. _____

17. _____

The answer is less than exhaust.

e. Is the individual maximizing utility? Should more, less, or the same amount be spent on X to maximize utility?

Since the individual is not spending all his income, he is not maximizing utility.

The answer is no.

Since the individual is not spending all his income, he can purchase more of good X and good Y thereby increasing his utility.

The answer is spend more on both goods.

3. Suppose that the price of good X is $10.00 and the price of good Y is $2.00. An individual whose income is $1,000.00 purchases a bundle of goods containing 40 units of good X and 300 units of good Y. The individual's marginal rate of substitution is 8.

a. What is the X-intercept of the individual's budget line?

18. _____

b. What is the Y-intercept of the individual's budget line?

19. _____

20. _____

c. Does the bundle exhaust the individual's income?

21. _____

d. Is the individual maximizing utility? Should more, less, or the same amount be spent on X to maximize utility?

22. _____

4. Suppose that the price of good X is $2.00 and the price of good Y is $4.00. An individual whose income is $1,000.00 purchases a bundle of goods containing 300 units of good X and 100 units of good Y. The individual's marginal rate of substitution is 0.5.

a. What is the X-intercept of the individual's budget line?

23. _____

b. What is the Y-intercept of the individual's budget line?

24. _____

25. _____

c. Does the bundle exhaust the individual's income?

26. _____

d. Is the individual maximizing utility? Should more, less, or the same amount be spent on X to maximze utility?

27. _____

5. Suppose that the price of good X is $4.00 and the price of good Y is $2.00. An individual whose income is $1,200.00 purchases a bundle of goods containing 100 units of good X and 400 units of good Y. The individual's marginal rate of substitution is 6.

a. What is the X-intercept of the individual's budget line?

28. _____

b. What is the Y-intercept of the individual's budget line?

29. _____

30. _____

c. Does the bundle exhaust the individual's income?

31. _____

d. Is the individual maximizing utility? Should more, less, or the same amount be spent on X to maximize utility?

32. _____

INCOME AND SUBSTITUTION EFFECTS

1. Initially the price of good X is $1.00, the price of good Y is $2.00, and income is $100.00. Income increases from $100.00 to $150.00. Good X is a normal good.

a. Plot the old and new budget lines on the diagram below.

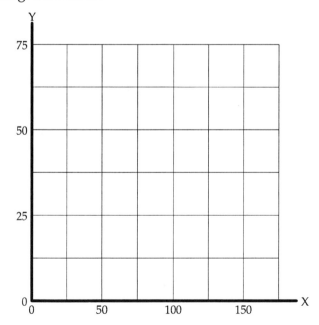

b. What happens to the slope of the budget line?

The slope of the budget line depends on the _____ ratio. Since neither the price of good X nor the price of good Y has changed, the slope is _____.

33. _____

34. _____

The answer is nothing.

c. Is there a substitution effect? As a result, does the utility maximizing quantity of X increase, decrease, or remain the same?

Since the slope of the budget line is unchanged, there is _____ substitution effect.

35. _____

The answer is no. The utility maximizing quantity of X is unaffected.

d. What happens to the X-intercept of the budget line?

The X-intercept of the budget line illustrates the situation when the consumer spends all his income on good _____. Initially, since the price of good X was $1.00 and income was $100.00, the X-intercept was _____. After income rises from $100.00 to $150.00, the X-intercept increases to _____.

36. _____

37. _____

38. _____

The answer is it increases from 100 to 150.

e. What happens to the Y-intercept of the budget line?

The _____ of the budget line illustrates the situation when the consumer spends all his income on good Y. Initially, since the price of good Y was $2.00 and income was $100.00, the Y-intercept was _____. After income rises from $100.00 to $150.00, the Y-intercept increases to _____.

39. _____

40. _____
41. _____

The answer is it increases from 50 to 75.

f. Is there an income effect? As a result, does the utility maximizing quantity of X increase, decrease, or remain the same?

42. _____   The budget line has shifted _____; consequently there is an income effect.

The answer is yes.

For a normal good when the budget line shifts outward, the utility maximizing quantity of the good
43. _____   _____; when the budget line shifts
44. _____   _____, the utility maximizing quantity of the good decreases. Since good X is normal and the budget line has shifted outward, the quantity of good
45. _____   X _____ as a consequence of the income effect.

The answer is it increases.

g. Accounting for both the income and substitution effects, how is the utility maximizing quantity of good X affected?

46. _____   Since there is _____ substitution effect and the income effect leads to the consumption of more X, the
47. _____   quantity of good X _____.

The answer is it increases.

- 72 -

2. Initially the price of good X is $1.00, the price of good Y is $2.00, and income is $100.00. Income decreases from $100.00 to $50.00. Good X is an inferior good.

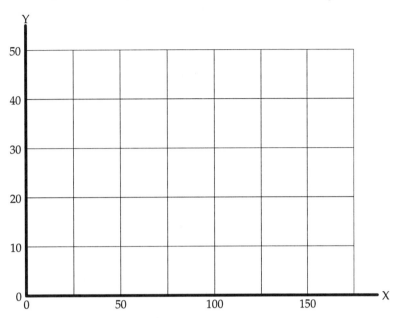

a. Plot the old and new budget lines on the above diagram.

b. What happens to the slope of the budget line?

The slope of the budget line depends on the price ratio. Since neither the price of good X nor the price of good Y has changed, the slope is _____.

48. _____

The answer is nothing.

c. Is there a substitution effect? As a result, does the utility maximizing quantity of X increase, decrease, or remain the same?

49. _____

Since the slope of the budget line is _____, there is no substitution effect.

The answer is no.

d. What happens to the X-intercept of the budget line?

50. _____

The _____ of the budget line illustrates the situation when the consumer spends all his income

51. _____

52. _____

on good X. Initially, since the price of good X was $1.00 and income was $100.00, the X-intercept was _____. After income falls from $100.00 to $50.00, the X-intercept decreases to _____.

The answer is it decreases from 100 to 50.

e. What happens to the Y-intercept of the budget line?

53. _____

54. _____

55. _____

The Y-intercept of the budget line illustrates the situation when the consumer spends all his income on good _____. Initially, since the price of good Y was $2.00 and income was $100.00, the Y-intercept was _____. After income falls from $100.00 to $50.00, the Y-intercept decreases to _____.

The answer is it decreases from 50 to 25.

f. Is there an income effect? As a result, does the utility maximizing quantity of X increase, decrease, or remain the same?

56. _____

The budget line has shifted _____; consequently, there is an income effect.

The answer is yes.

57. _____

58. _____

59. _____

For an inferior good when the budget line shifts outward, the utility maximizing quantity of the good _____; when the budget line shifts _____, the utility maximizing quantity of the good increases. Since good X is inferior and the budget line has shifted inward, the quantity of good X _____.

The answer is it increases.

g. Accounting for both the income and substitution effects how is the utility maximizing quantity of good X affected?

Since there is no substitution effect and the income effect leads to the consumption of more X, the quantity of good X _____.

60. _____

The answer is it increases.

3. Initially the price of good X is $1.00, the price of good Y is $2.00, and income is $100.00. The price of good X decreases from $1.00 to $.50. Good X is a normal good.

a. Plot the old and new budget lines on the above diagram.

b. What happens to the slope of the budget line?

61. _____

62. _____

63. _____

The slope of the budget line depends on the _____ ratio; the slope equals the negative of the price of good X divided by the price of good Y. Since the price of good X has _____, the price ratio has declined and the budget line is _____ steeply sloped.

The answer is it becomes less steeply sloped.

c. Is there a substitution effect? As a result, does the utility maximizing quantity of X increase, decrease, or remain the same?

64. _____   Since the slope of the budget line has _____, there is a substitution effect.

The answer is yes.

65. _____   Good X has become _____ expensive relative to good Y; as a consequence of the substitution effect, the utility maximizing quantity of good X

66. _____   _____.

The answer is it increases.

d. What happens to the X-intercept of the budget line?

The X-intercept of the budget line illustrates the situation when the consumer spends all his income
67. _____   on good _____. Initially, since the price of good X was $1.00 and income was $100.00, the X-
68. _____   intercept was _____. After the price of good X falls from $1.00 to $.50, the X-intercept increases to 200.

The answer is it increases from 100 to 200.

e. What happens to the Y-intercept of the budget line?

The Y-intercept of the budget line illustrates the situation when the consumer spends all his income
69. _____   on good _____. Initially, since the price of good Y was $2.00 and income was $100.00, the Y-
70. _____   intercept was _____. Since neither the price of good Y nor income has changed, the Y-intercept is unchanged.

The answer is nothing.

f. Is there an income effect? As a result, does the utility maximizing quantity of X increase, decrease, or remain the same?

The budget line has shifted outward; consequently there is an income effect.

The answer is yes.

71. _____

For a(n) _____ good when the budget line shifts outward, the utility maximizing quantity of the good increases; when the budget line shifts inward, the utility maximizing quantity of the good

72. _____

_____. Since good X is normal and the budget line has shifted outward, the quantity of good X

73. _____

_____ as a consequence of the income effect.

The answer is it increases.

g. Accounting for both the income and substitution effects how is the utility maximizing quantity of good X affected?

74. _____

Both the income and substitution effects lead to the consumption of _____ X. The utility maximizing quantity of good X increases.

The answer is it increases.

4. Initially the price of good X is $1.00, the price of good Y is $2.00, and income is $100.00. The price of good X increases from $1.00 to $2.00. Good X is a normal good.

75. _____

a. What happens to the slope of the budget line?

76. _____
77. _____

b. Is there a substitution effect? Does the quantity of X increase, decrease, or remain the same?

78. _____

c. What happens to the X-intercept of the budget line?

79. _____

d. What happens to the Y-intercept of the budget line?

80. _____
81. _____

e. Is there an income effect? Does the quantity of X increase, decrease, or remain the same?

82. _____

f. Accounting for both the income and substitution effects, how is the utility maximizing quantity of good X affected?

5. Initially the price of good X is $1.00, the price of good Y is $2.00, and income is $100.00. The price of good X increases from $1.00 to $2.00. Good X is an inferior good.

83. _____   a. What happens to the slope of the budget line?

84. _____   b. Is there a substitution effect? Does the quantity of X
85. _____   increase, decrease, or remain the same?

86. _____   c. What happens to the X-intercept of the budget line?

87. _____   d. What happens to the Y-intercept of the budget line?

88. _____   e. Is there an income effect? Does the quantity of X
89. _____   increase, decrease, or remain the same?

                     f. Accounting for both the income and substitution
                         effects, how is the utility maximizing quantity of
90. _____   good X affected?

6. Initially the price of good X is $1.00, the price of good Y is $2.00, and income is $100.00. The price of good X decreases from $1.00 to $.50. Good X is an inferior good.

91. _____   a. What happens to the slope of the budget line?

92. _____   b. Is there a substitution effect? Does the quantity of X
93. _____   increase, decrease, or remain the same?

94. _____   c. What happens to the X-intercept of the budget line?

95. _____   d. What happens to the Y-intercept of the budget line?

96. _____   e. Is there an income effect? Does the quantity of X
97. _____   increase, decrease, or remain the same?

                     f. Accounting for both the income and substitution
                         effects, how is the utility maximizing quantity of
98. _____   good X affected?

SHIFTS AND MOVEMENTS ALONG DEMAND CURVES

1. The income elasticity of demand is .50 and the price elasticity of demand is –.50. Initially income is $20,000, the price is $.60, and the quantity is 1,000. Income increases from $20,000 to $22,000.

    a. Will the demand curve shift? Does it shift to the right, left, or remain stationary?

99. _____
100. _____

    The demand curve can shift only if something other than the _____ of the good itself changes. Since income has risen, the demand curve will _____.

    The answer is yes.

101. _____
102. _____
103. _____

    Income rises from $20,000 to $22,000, a(n) _____ percent increase. Since the income elasticity of demand is .50, a 10 percent change in income causes a _____ percent change in the quantity. The demand curve will shift to the right by 5 percent of 1,000, which is _____.

    The answer is it shifts to the right by 50.

    b. Is there a change in demand?

104. _____
105. _____

    A change in demand refers to a(n) _____ of the demand curve. Since the demand curve has shifted to the right by 50, demand has _____ by 50.

    The answer is yes, an increase in demand.

    c. Will there be a movement along the demand curve? By how much do we move along the demand curve?

106. _____
107. _____

    A movement along the demand curve occurs only if the _____ of the good itself changes. Since the price is unchanged, there is _____ movement along the demand curve.

    The answer is no.

d. Is there a change in the quantity demanded?

108. _____

109. _____

A change in the quantity demanded refers to a movement _____ the demand curve. Since there has not been a movement along the demand curve, there has been no change in the _____ demanded.

The answer is no.

2. The income elasticity of demand is .50 and the price elasticity of demand is –.50. Initially income is $20,000, the price is $.60, and the quantity is 1,000. The price increases from $.60 to $.72.

a. Will the demand curve shift? Does it shift to the right, left, or remain stationary?

110. _____

111. _____

The demand curve can _____ only if something other than the price of the good itself changes. Since income has not changed, the demand curve will _____ shift.

The answer is no.

b. Is there a change in demand?

112. _____

113. _____

A change in demand refers to a(n) _____ of the demand curve. Since the demand curve has not shifted, there is _____ change in demand.

The answer is no.

c. Will there be a movement along the demand curve? By how much do we move along the demand curve?

114. _____

115. _____

A movement along the demand curve occurs only if the _____ of the good itself changes. Since the price has changed, there will be a movement _____ the demand curve.

The answer is yes.

116. _____

117. _____

118. _____

The price has increased from $.60 to $.72, which is a _____ percent increase. Since the price elasticity of demand is −.50, a 20 percent increase in the price will lead to a(n) _____ percent decrease in the quantity. The quantity decreases by 10 percent of 1,000, which is _____.

The answer is by a decrease of 100.

d. Is there a change in the quantity demanded?

119. _____

120. _____
121. _____

A change in the quantity demanded refers to a movement _____ the demand curve. There has been a movement along the demand curve because the price has _____; the quantity demanded has decreased by _____.

The answer is yes, a decrease of 100.

3. The income elasticity of demand is .50 and the price elasticity of demand is −1.00. Initially income is $20,000, the price is $.60, and the quantity is 1,000. The price decreases from $.60 to $.54.

122. _____
123. _____

a. Will the demand curve shift? Does it shift to the right, left, or remain stationary?

124. _____

b. Is there a change in demand?

125. _____
126. _____

c. Will there be a movement along the demand curve? By how much do we move along the demand curve?

127. _____

d. Is there a change in the quantity demanded?

4. The income elasticity of demand is 1.00 and the price elasticity of demand is –1.00. Initially income is $20,000, the price is $.60, and the quantity is 1,000. Income decreases from $20,000 to $15,000.

128. _____   a. Will the demand curve shift? Does it shift to the
129. _____   right, left, or remain stationary?

130. _____   b. Is there a change in demand?

131. _____   c. Will there be a movement along the demand curve?
132. _____   By how much do we move along the demand curve?

133. _____   d. Is there a change in the quantity demanded?

5. The income elasticity of demand is .50 and the price elasticity of demand is –1.00. Initially income is $20,000, the price is $.60, and the quantity is 1,000. Income increases from $20,000 to $24,000 and the price decreases from $.60 to $.48.

134. _____   a. Will the demand curve shift? Does it shift to the
135. _____   right, left, or remain stationary?

136. _____   b. Is there a change in demand?

137. _____   c. Will there be a movement along the demand curve?
138. _____   By how much do we move along the demand curve?

139. _____   d. Is there a change in the quantity demanded?

ANSWERS

1. X
2. 100
3. Y-intercept
4. 300
5. 360
6. 240
7. 600
8. Utility
9. 2
10. better
11. X-intercept
12. 80
13. Y
14. 200
15. 300
16. 80
17. less than
18. 100
19. 500
20. Yes
21. No
22. Consume more X
23. 500
24. 250
25. Yes
26. Yes
27. Consume the same
28. 300
29. 600
30. Yes
31. No
32. Consume more X
33. price
34. unchange
35. no
36. X
37. 100
38. 150
39. Y-intercept
40. 50
41. 75
42. outward

43. increases
44. inward
45. increases
46. no
47. increases
48. unchanged
49. unchanged
50. X-intercept
51. 100
52. 50
53. Y
54. 50
55. 25
56. inward
57. decreases
58. inward
59. increases
60. increases
61. price
62. fallen
63. less
64. changed
65. less
66. increases
67. X
68. 100
69. Y
70. 50
71. normal
72. decreases
73. increases
74. more
75. More steep
76. Yes
77. Decreases
78. Decreases
79. No change
80. Yes
81. Decreases
82. Decreases
83. Less steep
84. Yes

85. Decreases
86. Decreases
87. No change
88. Yes
89. Increases
90. One cannot tell.
91. Less steep
92. Yes
93. Increases
94. Increases
95. No change
96. Yes
97. Decreases
98. One cannot tell.
99. price
100. shift
101. 10
102. 5
103. 50
104. shift
105. increased
106. price
107. no
108. along
109. quantity
110. shift
111. not
112. shift
113. no
114. price
115. along
116. 20
117. 10
118. 100
119. along
120. changed
121. 100
122. No
123. Stationary
124. No
125. Yes
126. Increase of 100

127. Yes
128. Yes
129. Leftward by 250
130. Yes
131. No

132. No change
133. No
134. Yes
135. Rightward by 100
136. Yes

137. Yes
138. Increase of 200
139. Yes

PART 3

PRODUCTION, COSTS, AND SUPPLY

CHAPTER 5

PRODUCTION

LEARNING OBJECTIVES

- A firm's production function relates the inputs a firm uses to the output it produces.
- Marginal physical product of labor equals the additional output that can be produced from one additional unit of labor while holding all other inputs constant.
- An isoquant illustrates all the combinations of labor and capital that will produce a given level of output.
- The rate of technical substitution reflects how the firm can substitute capital for labor while keeping the level of output constant.
- Returns to scale indicate what happens to output when all inputs are changed by the same proportion.

WALKING TOUR SUMMARIES

PRODUCTION FUNCTION

1. _____

A firm's production function summarizes what the firm knows about using inputs to produce _____:

$$\text{Quantity of Output} = Q = f(K, L, M, ...)$$

K equals the units of capital used, L units of labor, and M units of raw materials. It is convenient to simplify the presentation by focusing attention on the capital and labor:

$$Q = f(K, L)$$

MARGINAL PHYSICAL PRODUCTIVITY: WHAT HAPPENS TO OUTPUT WHEN THE FIRM CHANGES ONE INPUT WITHOUT CHANGING ANY OTHER INPUTS

2. _____

A firm's marginal physical productivity of labor equals the change in output resulting from the use of one additional unit of labor while keeping all other _____ constant.   This can be expressed more mathematically:

$$\text{Marginal Physical Productivity of Labor} = MP_L$$
$$= \frac{\text{Change in Output}}{\text{Change in Labor Input}}$$

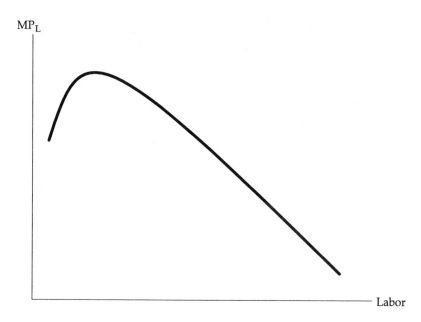

Figure 5.1: *Marginal Productivity of Labor*

DIMINISHING MARGINAL PHYSICAL PRODUCTIVITY

3. _____

As a firm uses more and more labor without changing the amount of other inputs used, the marginal physical productivity of labor will _____.

AVERAGE PHYSICAL PRODUCTIVITY

A firm's average physical productivity of labor refers to how much output is produced per unit of labor; that is, average physical productivity equals the _____ of output to labor:

4. _____

$$\text{Average Physical Productivity of Labor} = AP_L$$
$$= \frac{\text{Output}}{\text{Labor Input}}$$

THE TOTAL PRODUCTIVITY, MARGINAL PRODUCTIVITY, AND AVERAGE PRODUCTIVITY CURVES

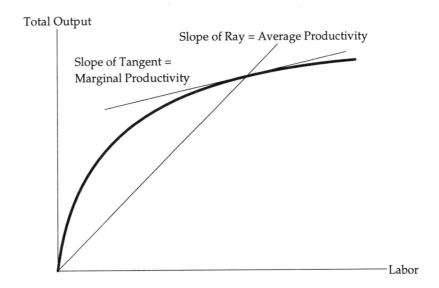

Figure 5.2: *Total, Marginal, and Average Productivity*

The total productivity of labor curve illustrates how a firm's total production of output is affected when it uses more and more labor without changing any _____ inputs. At low levels of labor usage, output increases rapidly as additional labor is used, but eventually due to _____ marginal productivity, the increase in output will slow. The firm may even reach a point where it cannot produce more output. Using additional labor beyond this point would cause output to decrease. The marginal physical productivity of labor equals the _____ of the total labor productivity curve. The slope illustrates how output will change when the firm uses one additional unit

5. _____

6. _____

7. _____

8. _____ of labor. The _____ productivity of labor equals the slope of the ray connecting the origin and the relevant point on the total productivity curve.

ISOQUANT MAPS: HOW INPUTS CAN BE SUBSTITUTED FOR EACH OTHER TO KEEP OUTPUT CONSTANT

9. _____

10. _____

11. _____

12. _____

13. _____

To construct an isoquant, first choose a level of _____ _____ and then find all the different combinations of capital and labor that will allow the firm to produce that level of output. An isoquant is just a contour line of the _____ function. Any two combinations of labor and capital lying on the _____ isoquant will produce the same level of output. A combination on an isoquant will produce more output than a combination lying _____ the curve. Any combination lying above an isoquant will produce _____ output than a combination on the curve.

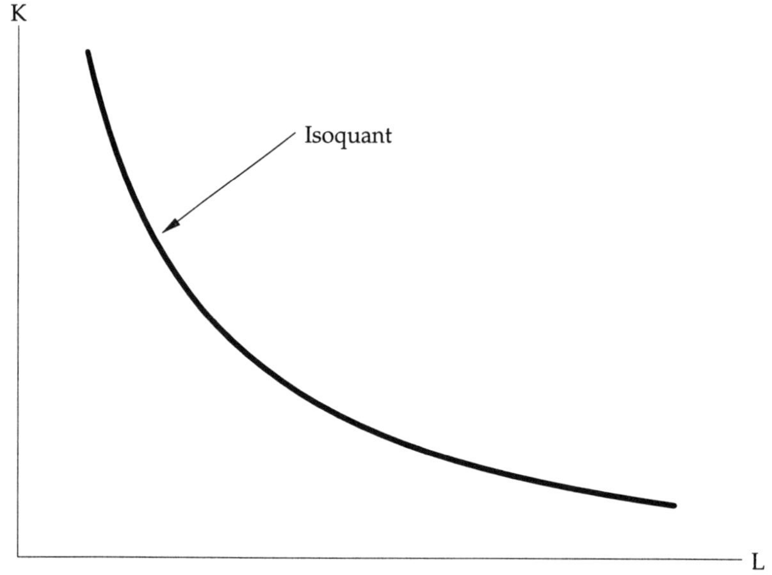

Figure 5.3: *Isoquant*

RATE OF TECHNICAL SUBSTITUTION

A firm's rate of technical substitution of labor for capital equals the amount by which capital can be reduced when one more unit of labor is used in order to keep the quantity

14. _____ produced _____:

$$\text{Rate of Technical Substitution} = \text{RTS}$$
$$= \frac{\text{Change in Capital}}{\text{Change in Labor}}$$

while holding output constant. A firm's rate of technical substitution depends upon the amount of capital and labor it is now using. As the firm substitutes more and more labor for capital, its rate of technical substitution _____. Economists call this diminishing rate of technical substitution.

15. _____

ISOQUANTS AND THE RATE OF TECHNICAL SUBSTITUTION

16. _____

The _____ of a firm's isoquant equals the ratio by which the firm can substitute labor for capital while keeping production constant. The slope of a firm's isoquant and its rate of _____ substitution represent the same thing.

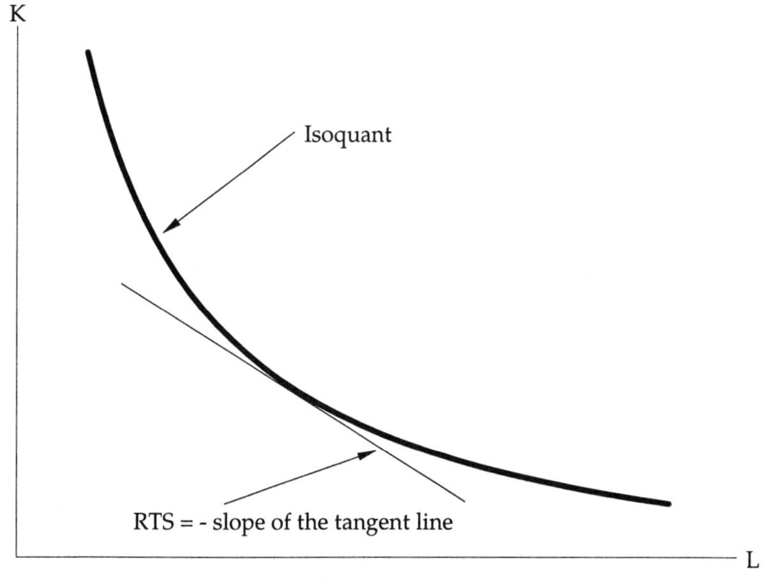

17. _____

Figure 5.4: *Rate of Technical Substitution*

RETURNS TO SCALE: HOW OUTPUT IS AFFECTED WHEN ALL INPUTS ARE INCREASED SIMULTANEOUSLY

18. _____ A production function exhibits constant returns to scale, if a doubling of all inputs exactly _____ output;

19. _____ _____ returns to scale, if a doubling of all inputs less than doubles output; and increasing returns to scale,

20. _____ if a doubling of all inputs _____ than doubles output.

CHANGES IN TECHNOLOGY

Technological innovation allows a firm to produce the same amount of output with fewer inputs. Therefore, technological change causes a firm's isoquants to shift

21. _____ _____, toward the origin.

MULTIPLE-CHOICE QUESTIONS

22. _____ A production function describes how
   a. an individual can turn goods into utility.
   b. an individual can turn inputs into utility.
   c. a firm can turn goods into output.
   d. a firm can turn inputs into output.
   e. a and d.

23. _____ A firm's marginal physical productivity of labor equals
   a. the change in the firm's output resulting from the use of one additional unit of labor without changing any other inputs.
   b. the firm's total output divided by the units of labor used.
   c. the ratio of the change in output to the change in labor input without changing any other inputs.
   d. the ratio of total output to labor input.
   e. a and c.

24. _____ As a firm uses more and more labor without changing any other inputs, its marginal physical productivity of labor eventually will
   a. increase.
   b. decrease.
   c. remain constant.
   d. equal marginal cost.
   e. b and d.

25. _____ A firm's average physical productivity of labor equals
    a. the change in the firm's output resulting from the use of one additional unit of labor without changing any other inputs.
    b. the firm's total output divided by the units of labor used.
    c. the ratio of the change in output to the change in labor input without changing any other inputs.
    d. the ratio of marginal physical productivity to labor input.
    e. b and d.

26. _____ A firm's total product of labor curve
    a. relates total output to all inputs used.
    b. is a contour line of the production function.
    c. illustrates all the combinations of capital and labor that will produce a constant level of output.
    d. relates output to the amount of labor used, keeping all other inputs constant.
    e. a and b.

27. _____ Graphically, a firm's marginal physical productivity of labor equals the slope of the
    a. total product of labor curve at the relevant point.
    b. straight line connecting the origin with the relevant point on the total product of labor curve.
    c. average productivity of labor curve at the relevant point.
    d. straight line connecting the origin with the relevant point on the average productivity of labor curve.
    e. a and c.

28. _____ Graphically, a firm's average physical productivity of labor equals the slope of the
    a. total product of labor curve at the relevant point.
    b. straight line connecting the origin with the relevant point on the total product of labor curve.
    c. average productivity of labor curve at the relevant point.
    d. straight line connecting the origin with the relevant point on the average productivity of labor curve.
    e. a and c.

29. _____ A firm's isoquant
   a. relates output to the amount of labor used keeping all other inputs constant.
   b. relates total output to all inputs used.
   c. is a contour line of the production function.
   d. illustrates all the combinations of capital and labor that will produce a constant level of output.
   e. c and d.

30. _____ A firm's rate of technical substitution of labor for capital
   a. equals the amount by which capital can be reduced when one more unit of labor is used while keeping the level of production constant.
   b. equals the ratio of capital used to labor used.
   c. reflects the ratio by which capital and labor can be substituted in order to keep output constant.
   d. equals the ratio of total output to inputs.
   e. a and c.

31. _____ A firm's rate of technical substitution
   a. always increases whenever labor and capital are increased by the same percentage.
   b. always decreases whenever labor and capital are increased by the same percentage.
   c. depends on the amount of labor and capital being used presently.
   d. is constant.
   e. a and c.

32. _____ Graphically, a firm's rate of technical substitution is reflected by the slope of the
   a. isoquant at the relevant point.
   b. line connecting the origin with the relevant point on the isoquant.
   c. production function at the relevant point.
   d. line connecting the origin with the relevant point on the production function.
   e. a and d.

33. _____ As a firm moves along an isoquant substituting more and more labor for capital, the rate of technical substitution
    a. typically increases.
    b. typically decreases.
    c. always remains the same.
    d. may increase or remain constant, but cannot decrease.
    e. always increases.

34. _____ Returns to scale indicate how a firm's total output changes whenever
    a. only one input changes.
    b. all but one input changes.
    c. all inputs change.
    d. no inputs change.
    e. none of the above.

35. _____ If a firm's production function exhibits increasing returns to scale, a doubling of all inputs will
    a. less than double output.
    b. more than double output.
    c. exactly double output.
    d. not affect output.
    e. increase the rate of technical substitution.

36. _____ If a firm's production function exhibits constant returns to scale, a doubling of all inputs will
    a. less than double output.
    b. more than double output.
    c. exactly double output.
    d. not affect output.
    e. increase the rate of technical substitution.

RUNNING GLOSSARY

37. _____ Firm: any organization that turns _____ into outputs.

38. _____ _____ function: the mathematical relationship between inputs and outputs.

39. _____ Marginal physical productivity: the _____ output that can be produced by one more unit of a particular input while holding all other inputs constant.

40. _____ Average productivity: the _____ of total output produced to the quantity of a particular input employed.

41. _____ _____ map: a contour map of a firm's production function.

   Isoquant: a curve that shows the various combinations of
42. _____ _____ that will produce the same amount of output.

43. _____ Marginal rate of _____ substitution: the negative of the slope of an isoquant. This shows the amount by which
44. _____ capital input can be reduced while holding the _____ constant when one more unit of labor input is added.

45. _____ _____ to scale: the rate at which output increases in response to proportional increases in all inputs.

   Fixed proportions production function: a production function in which the inputs must be used in a(n)
46. _____ _____ratio to one another.

   Technical progress: a shift in the production function that allows a given output level to be produced using
47. _____ _____ inputs.

ANSWERS

1. output	17. technical	33. b
2. inputs	18. doubles	34. c
3. diminish	19. decreasing	35. b
4. ratio	20. more	36. c
5. other	21. in	37. inputs
6. diminishing	22. d	38. Production
7. slope	23. e	39. additional
8. average	24. b	40. ratio
9. output	25. b	41. Isoquant
10. production	26. d	42. inputs
11. same	27. a	43. technical
12. below	28. b	44. output
13. more	29. e	45. Returns
14. constant	30. e	46. fixed
15. decreases	31. c	47. less
16. slope	32. a	

CHAPTER 6

COSTS

LEARNING OBJECTIVES

- Opportunity costs reflect what must be forgone when producing a good or service.
- A firm's economic profit is the difference between its total revenues and its total economic costs.
- When producing a given level of output at the lowest possible cost, the firm's rate of technical substitution will equal the wage-rental ratio.
- Average cost equals total cost divided by the quantity of output produced.
- Marginal cost equals the additional cost incurred when one additional unit of output is produced.
- In the long run, a firm can vary both labor and capital; in the short run, a firm can vary labor, but not capital.
- In the short run, the average total cost curve is typically U-shaped; the short-run marginal cost curve and the short-run average cost curve intersect at minimum short-run average total cost.
- The cost of producing a given level of output in the short run cannot be less than the cost in the long run.

WALKING TOUR SUMMARIES

BASIC CONCEPTS OF COSTS

1. _____ _____

2. _____ _____

3. _____

4. _____

The production of any good requires the use of resources. _____ cost refers to the other goods forgone when we use resources to produce the good in question. The _____'s concept of cost refers to the firm's out-of-pocket expenses. That is, what the firm must pay to others for using the resources it employs. _____ cost refers to what the firm must pay for the resources it uses to keep those resources employed at the firm. Putting it differently, economic cost is the _____ someone else would pay to use the resources the firm employs. That is, the remuneration the resources would receive in their best alternative use.

5. _____ _____ Economic profit equals total revenue less cost. Economic profit of an owner-operated firm equals the income the owner receives from the firm

6. _____ _____ what is necessary to keep the owner operating

7. _____ his firm; that is, less the _____ someone would pay the owner to work elsewhere.

COST-MINIMIZING INPUT CHOICE

Once the firm decides upon its level of production, the firm will produce its output using the input combination

8. _____ that _____ total costs. The firm produces its chosen level of output in the least costly way whenever its rate of

9. _____ _____ substitution equals the ratio of the wage and rental rates. To understand why, recall that a(n)

10. _____ _____ represents all the combinations of labor and capital that can produce a given level of output. We wish to find that combination of labor and capital, that point on the isoquant, which minimizes the firm's total costs. In light of our previous assumption that a firm's only inputs are labor and capital, a firm's total costs are:

$$\text{Total Costs} = TC = wL + vK$$
$$\text{where } w = \text{wage rate of labor}$$
$$v = \text{rental rate of capital}$$

11. _____ The combinations of labor and capital that keep total costs constant lie on a straight line with _____ equal to $-w/v$. The least costly way to produce the firm's chosen level of production is the point on the isoquant that is

12. _____ _____ to the equal total cost curve. In this situation, all less costly combinations of labor and capital lie

13. _____ _____ the isoquant. This means that the firm cannot reduce its total costs without decreasing its level of production.

14. _____ A firm's _____ path illustrates how the cost-minimizing combination of labor and capital changes with the firm's level of output changes. To construct the expansion path, find the cost-minimizing combination of

15. _____ labor and capital for each level of _____. The expansion path is the locus of these points. A negatively sloped expansion path indicates that higher levels of

16. _____ production result in using _____ of one input.
17. _____ Economists call such an input _____.

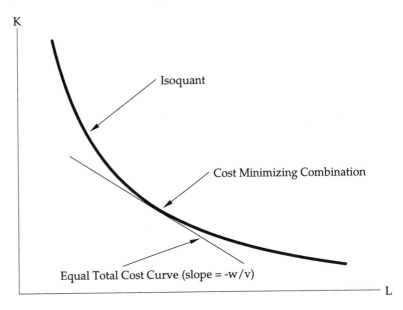

Figure 6.1: *Cost-Minimizing Combination*

TOTAL COST CURVE

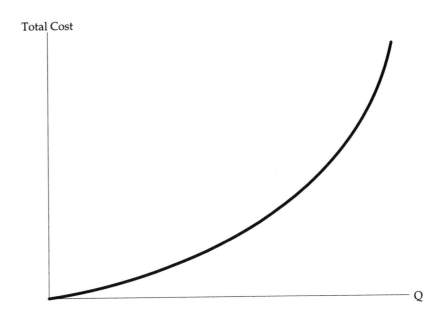

Figure 6.2: *Total Cost Curve*

18. _____ A firm's total cost curve illustrates the costs the firm incurs when it produces different levels of _____. The total cost curve passes through the origin. If the firm produces

19. _____

20. _____

21. _____

22. _____

23. _____

no output, it uses no inputs and its total costs are _____. Also, the total cost curve is always upward sloping. To produce more output, the firm must employ more inputs, which _____ its total costs. The total cost curve is a straight line whenever the production function exhibits _____ returns to scale; inputs and hence costs expand proportionally as output rises. The total cost curve is concave whenever the production function exhibits _____ returns to scale; inputs and hence costs expand more than proportionally as output rises. Last, the total cost curve is convex with _____ returns to scale.

MARGINAL COST CURVE

24. _____

A firm's marginal cost equals the change in total cost resulting from the production of _____ additional unit of output:

$$\text{Marginal Cost} = \text{MC}$$
$$= \frac{\text{Change in Total Cost}}{\text{Change in Quantity}}$$

25. _____
26. _____
27. _____

28. _____

Graphically, marginal cost is the slope of the total cost curve. It is constant when the production function exhibits _____ returns to scale. Marginal cost is increasing with _____ returns to scale and decreasing with _____ returns to scale. If the production function exhibits increasing returns to scale for low levels of production and decreasing returns to scale for high levels, the marginal cost curve will be _____-shaped.

AVERAGE COST CURVE

29. _____

A firm's average cost equals its total costs divided by the _____; that is, average cost is the ratio of total costs to quantity:

$$\text{Average Cost} = \text{AC}$$
$$= \frac{\text{Total Cost}}{\text{Quantity}}$$

Graphically, average cost equals the slope of the ray from the origin to the total cost curve.

- 102 -

Total Cost

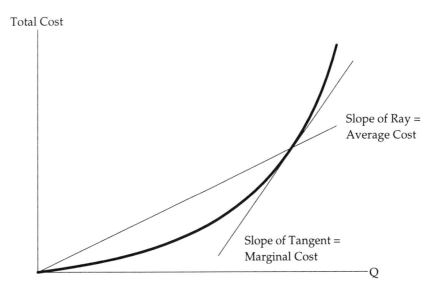

Figure 6.3: *Total, Marginal, and Average Cost*

AVERAGE AND MARGINAL COST CURVES

If the marginal cost curve is U-shaped, the average total cost curve will be U-shaped also. When the average cost curve is falling, marginal cost must be _____ 30. than average cost; if the average cost of production decreases when an additional unit is produced, the cost of producing the additional unit itself (marginal cost) must be _____ than the average. Similarly, when average 31. cost is rising, marginal cost must _____ average cost; 32. if the average cost of production increases when an additional unit is produced, the cost of producing the additional unit itself (the marginal cost) must be _____ than the average. Since marginal cost must be 33. less than average cost when the average is falling and marginal cost must be greater than average cost when the average is rising, marginal cost must _____ average 34. cost when the average is at its minimum. The marginal and average cost curves _____ at the point of minimum 35. average cost.

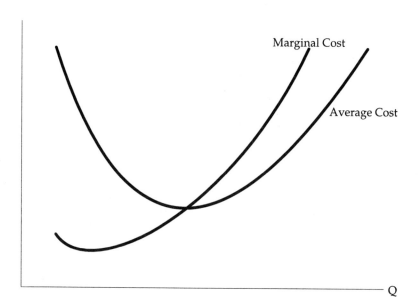

Figure 6.4: *Marginal and Average Cost Curves*

DISTINCTION BETWEEN THE SHORT RUN AND THE LONG RUN

36. _____

37. _____

In the _____ run, the firm can vary all input while in the short run some inputs are fixed. Typically, _____ is assumed to be fixed. In the short run, total costs can be divided into two components:

$$STC = SFC + SVC$$

38. _____

39. _____

40. _____

Costs that are fixed in the short run are called _____ costs, denoted by SFC. Similarly, economists call costs associated with the variable inputs _____ costs, denoted by SVC. Fixed costs are constant, unaffected by the level produced. Variable costs, on the other hand, change as the level of production changes. Short-run average total cost equals short-run total cost divided by _____:

$$SAC = \frac{STC}{Q} = \frac{SFC}{Q} + \frac{SVC}{Q}$$

41. _____

42. _____

43. _____

Typically, the short-run average total cost curve is _____-shaped. The short-run marginal cost curve eventually becomes _____ sloping as a result of diminishing marginal productivity. These two curves intersect at the point of _____ average total cost.

THE RELATIONSHIP BETWEEN SHORT-RUN AND LONG-RUN CURVES

44. _____ In the long run, the firm can change _____ its inputs.
45. _____ In the short run, the firm can change only _____ inputs. Because the firm has more flexibility in the long run than in the short run, long-run costs are typically
46. _____ _____ than short-run costs.

SHIFTS IN COST CURVES

Cost curves shift whenever any relevant economic factor changes. For example, whenever the price of an input rises, a firm's cost curves will be affected. Technological innovations have played a major factor in reducing firm costs. Also, when a firm produces several different products, the production of one product might reduce the cost of producing another product. This phenomenon is
47. _____ called economies of _____.

MULTIPLE-CHOICE QUESTIONS

48. _____ Opportunity cost of producing a good refers to
    a. the goods that must be forgone in order to produce the good in question.
    b. the out-of-pocket expenses a firm incurs when producing the good.
    c. the remuneration that must be made in order to keep all the resources used to produce the good in place.
    d. the most someone else would pay to use the resources now producing the good.
    e. the out-of-pocket payments the firm makes for the resources used to produce the good.

49. _____ The accountant's cost of producing a good refers to
  a. the goods that must be forgone in order to produce the good in question.
  b. the remuneration that must be made in order to keep all the resources used to produce the good in place.
  c. the most someone else would pay to use the resources now producing the good.
  d. the out-of-pocket payments the firm makes for the resources used to produce the good.
  e. b and d.

50. _____ The economist's cost of producing a good refers to
  a. the goods that must be forgone in order to produce the good in question.
  b. the out-of-pocket expenses a firm incurs when producing the good.
  c. the remuneration that must be made in order to keep all the resources used to produce the good in place.
  d. the most someone else would pay to use the resources now producing the good.
  e. c and d.

51. _____ The economic profit of an owner-operated firm equals
  a. total revenues less economic costs.
  b. total revenue less the firm's out-of-pocket costs.
  c. the income the owner receives from the firm less what is necessary to keep the owner operating his firm.
  d. the income the owner receives from the firm less the most someone else would pay the owner to work elsewhere.
  e. a, c, and d.

52. _____ A firm's equal total cost curve
  a. reflects all the combinations of labor and capital that will produce a given level of output.
  b. reflects all the combinations of labor and capital that cost the firm the same amount.
  c. is upward sloping.
  d. is horizontal.
  e. b and d.

53. _____ The slope of a firm's equal total cost curve
   a. reflects the ratio of the wage rate to the rental rate for capital.
   b. reflects the firm's marginal rate of substitution.
   c. equals zero.
   d. reflects the price of the good produced.
   e. a and d.

54. _____ In order to produce a given amount of output at the lowest possible cost, a firm will choose the input combination at which
   a. its rate of technical substitution equals the wage-rental ratio.
   b. its ratio of labor to capital used equals the wage-rental ratio.
   c. its ratio of the average labor productivity to the average capital productivity equals the wage-rental ratio.
   d. the amount of labor used is minimized.
   e. b and d.

55. _____ A firm's expansion path illustrates
   a. all the combinations of labor and capital that will produce a given level of output.
   b. the total costs a firm incurs producing each level of output.
   c. the cost-minimizing combinations of labor and capital for each level of output.
   d. the firm's marginal cost curve.
   e. c and d.

56. _____ If an input is inferior, a firm's expansion path will be
   a. horizontal.
   b. upward sloping.
   c. downward sloping.
   d. U-shaped.
   e. impossible to describe without additional information.

57. _____ A firm's total cost curve
   a. cannot be downward sloping.
   b. is always downward sloping.
   c. is always horizontal.
   d. may be upward sloping, downward sloping, or horizontal.
   e. is impossible to describe without additional information.

58. _____ If a firm's production function exhibits increasing returns to scale, the total cost curve is
   a. a straight upward sloping line.
   b. an upward sloping curve that bends downward.
   c. an upward sloping curve that bends upward.
   d. a downward sloping curve.
   e. impossible to describe without additional information.

59. _____ If a firm's production function exhibits constant returns to scale, the total cost curve is
   a. a straight upward sloping line.
   b. an upward sloping curve that bends downward.
   c. an upward sloping curve that bends upward.
   d. a downward sloping curve.
   e. impossible to describe without additional information.

60. _____ A firm's marginal cost equals
   a. the change in total cost resulting from the production of one additional unit of output.
   b. the ratio of total cost to output.
   c. the ratio of the change in a firm's total cost to a change in output.
   d. average cost at all levels of production.
   e. a and c.

61. _____ Graphically, a firm's marginal cost equals the slope of
   a. its average cost curve at the relevant point.
   b. the straight line connecting the origin with the relevant point on its average cost curve.
   c. its total cost curve at the relevant point.
   d. the straight line connecting the origin with the relevant point on its total cost curve.
   e. a and c.

62. _____ In the short run, a firm
   a. can vary all inputs.
   b. can vary only some inputs.
   c. can vary no inputs.
   d. cannot change its level of production.
   e. c and d.

63. _____ In the long run, a firm
   a. can vary all inputs.
   b. can vary only some inputs.
   c. can vary no inputs.
   d. cannot change its level of production.
   e. c and d.

64. _____ Costs associated with those inputs that a firm cannot vary in the short run are called
   a. total costs.
   b. accountant's costs.
   c. variable costs.
   d. fixed costs.
   e. b and d.

65. _____ Costs associated with those inputs that a firm can vary in the short run are called
   a. total costs.
   b. accountant's costs.
   c. variable costs.
   d. fixed costs.
   e. b and d.

66. _____ In the short run, a firm's average total cost curve is typically
   a. upward sloping.
   b. downward sloping.
   c. flat.
   d. U-shaped.
   e. upward sloping or flat.

67. _____ If a firm's marginal cost is greater than its average cost, its
   a. average cost curve must be falling.
   b. average cost curve must be rising.
   c. average cost curve may be rising, falling, or flat.
   d. marginal cost curve must be falling.
   e. marginal cost curve must be rising.

68. _____ If a firm's marginal cost is less than average cost, its
   a. average cost curve must be falling.
   b. average cost curve must be rising.
   c. average cost curve may be rising, falling, or flat.
   d. marginal cost curve must be falling.
   e. marginal cost curve must be rising.

69. _____ A firm's average cost curve and marginal cost curve intersect at the point of minimum
    a. marginal cost.
    b. average cost.
    c. total cost.
    d. average variable cost.
    e. a and b.

70. _____ A firm's short-run costs are
    a. always less than its long-run costs.
    b. never less than its long-run costs.
    c. sometimes less than its long-run costs and sometimes greater than its long-run costs.
    d. unrelated to its long-run costs.
    e. always greater than its long-run costs.

RUNNING GLOSSARY

71. _____ Opportunity cost: the cost of a good or service as measured by the alternative uses that are _____ by producing the good or service.

72. _____ _____ cost: the concept that goods or services cost what was paid for them.

73. _____ _____ cost: the concept that goods or services cost the amount required to keep them in their present use; the amount that they would be worth in their next best alternative use.

74. _____ Wage rate: the cost of hiring one _____ for one hour.

75. _____ _____ rate: the cost of hiring one machine for one hour.

76. _____ Economic _____: the difference between a firm's total revenues and its total economic costs.

77. _____ Expansion path: the locus of cost-minimizing _____ combinations a firm will choose to produce various levels of output (when the prices of inputs are held constant).

78. _____ Average cost: total costs divided by _____.

79. _____ Marginal cost: the additional cost of producing one _____ unit of output.

80. _____ _____ run: the period of time in which a firm must consider some inputs absolutely fixed in making its decisions.

81. _____ Long run: the period of time in which a firm may consider _____ of its inputs to be variable in making its decisions.

82. _____ Fixed costs: cost associated with inputs that are fixed in the _____ run.

83. _____ _____ costs: costs associated with inputs that can be varied in the short run.

84. _____ Economies of scope: exist when a firm produces more than a single product and the production of one product _____ the costs of producing other product(s).

ANSWERS

1. Opportunity	29. quantity	57. a
2. accountant	30. less	58. b
3. Economic	31. less	59. a
4. most	32. exceed	60. e
5. economic	33. greater	61. c
6. less	34. equal	62. b
7. most	35. intersect	63. a
8. minimizes	36. long	64. d
9. technical	37. capital	65. c
10. isoquant	38. fixed	66. d
11. slope	39. variable	67. b
12. tangent	40. quantity	68. a
13. below	41. U	69. b
14. expansion	42. upward	70. b
15. production	43. minimum	71. forgone
16. less	44. all	72. Accounting
17. inferior	45. variable	73. Economic
18. output	46. less	74. worker
19. zero	47. scope	75. Rental
20. increases	48. a	76. profits
21. constant	49. d	77. input
22. increasing	50. e	78. output
23. decreasing	51. e	79. more
24. one	52. b	80. Short
25. constant	53. a	81. all
26. decreasing	54. a	82. short
27. increasing	55. c	83. Variable
28. U	56. c	84. reduces

CHAPTER 7

PROFIT MAXIMIZATION AND SUPPLY

LEARNING OBJECTIVES
- Marginal revenue equals the additional revenue a firm receives when it sells one additional unit of output.
- Marginal cost equals the additional cost a firm incurs when it produces one additional unit of output.
- When a firm maximizes profit, its marginal revenue equals its marginal cost.
- When a firm is a price taker, its marginal revenue equals the price.
- When a firm is not a price taker, an increase in production causes the price to fall and its marginal revenue is less than the price.
- When a firm is a price taker, its short-run supply curve will be its short-run marginal cost curve as long as the price exceeds average variable cost.

WALKING TOUR SUMMARIES

PROFIT MAXIMIZATION

Economists typically assume that the goal of a firm is to maximize profits:

$$\text{Profits} = \text{Total Revenue} + \text{Total Costs}$$
$$= \quad TR \quad + \quad TC$$

1. _____ Total revenue equals price times _____:

$$TR = P \times Q$$

PROFIT MAXIMIZATION AND MARGINALISM

2. _____ Marginal _____ equals the additional revenue the firm obtains from the sale of one additional unit of
3. _____ output. Marginal _____ equals the additional cost the firm incurs from the production of one additional unit of output. To maximize profits the firm will produce the level

4. _____ of output at which marginal revenue _____
5. _____ marginal cost. Whenever marginal revenue _____ marginal cost, the production and sale of one additional unit of output will increase total revenues more than total costs. Therefore profits will rise with additional production. Alternatively, whenever marginal revenue is less than
6. _____ marginal cost, profits will _____ with reduced production. To maximize profits, marginal revenue must
7. _____ _____ marginal cost.

MARGINAL REVENUE

8. _____ If a firm is a price _____, the firm's output decision does not affect the price. In this case, the firm's marginal
9. _____ revenue _____ the price. Whenever the firm produces one additional unit of output, its total revenues
10. _____ rise by an amount _____ to the price.

On the other hand, if the price falls whenever the firm
11. _____ increases production, marginal revenue will be _____ than the price. To understand why assume that the quantity is initially 50 units and that the sale of one additional unit causes the price to fall from $1.00 to $.99. Recall that
12. _____ marginal revenue equals the change in total _____ resulting from the sale of one additional unit of production. The sale of one additional unit of production affects total revenue in two ways:

1. The sale of the additional unit itself causes total revenues to rise by an amount equal to the price. The sale of the 51st unit by itself produces $.99 of additional revenues.

2. The sale of the additional unit causes the price to fall from $1.00 to $.99. The lower price means that the firm will collect fewer revenues from the other units sold. Revenues collected from the other 50 units decrease from $50.00 (50 × $1.00) to $49.50 (50 × $.99).

As a consequence of the second effect, marginal revenue is
13. _____ less than the _____ .

MARGINAL REVENUE AND PRICE ELASTICITY

To understand the relationship between marginal revenue and elasticity of demand, recall that the elasticity of demand indicates how sensitive the quantity demanded is to a change in the price:

$$e_{Q,P} = \frac{\text{Percent Change in Quantity}}{\text{Percent Change in Price}}$$

Total revenue equals price times quantity:

$$TR = P \times Q.$$

If demand is inelastic, marginal revenue will be negative.

14. _____ While a fall in the price will _____ the quantity, it will not increase it by "very much" when demand is

15. _____ inelastic. Hence, total revenues will _____. Marginal revenue equals the change in total revenues resulting from the sale of one additional unit of output. Since total revenues fall as the quantity increases, marginal

16. _____ revenue must be _____. On the other hand, if

17. _____ demand is elastic, marginal revenue will be _____.

MARGINAL REVENUE CURVE

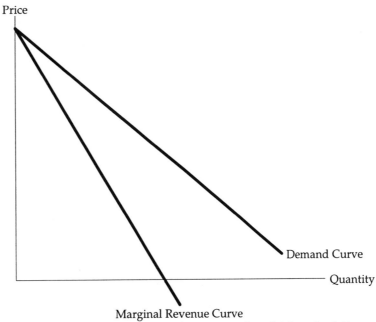

Figure 7.1: *Downward Sloping Demand and Marginal Revenue*

18. _____

19. _____

20. _____

21. _____

Every demand curve has a marginal revenue curve associated with it. The demand curve can be thought of as the _____ revenue curve. The demand curve illustrates the revenue per unit (that is, the price) yielded by alternative output choices. Whenever the demand curve is downward sloping, additional production causes average revenue to _____. The sale of an additional unit of output causes average revenue to fall. The extra revenue produced by the additional unit sold must be _____ than the average. Hence, when the demand curve is downward sloping the marginal revenue curve lies _____ the demand curve.

ALTERNATIVES TO PROFIT MAXIMIZATION

22. _____

23. _____

Other hypotheses to explain firm behavior have been advanced. Baumol suggested that _____ maximization may better explain firm behavior. Revenue maximizing firms would expand output beyond profit maximizing levels. Another alternative, the markup pricing hypothesis, appears to be quite similar to _____ maximization. Evidence suggests that markups vary within a business cycle just as profit maximization would suggest. Consequently, markup pricing may very well be consistent with profit maximization.

SHORT-RUN SUPPLY BY A PRICE-TAKING FIRM

24. _____

25. _____

26. _____

To maximize profits a firm produces the level of output at which marginal revenue _____ marginal cost. A price-taking firm's marginal revenue equals the _____. Putting both parts together, a profit-maximizing, price-taking firm produces the level of output at which _____ equals marginal cost. Therefore, the firm's individual supply curve is its marginal cost curve.

27. _____

28. _____

Before moving on we must amend this last statement to cover those situations in which the price is "very low." If the price falls below the firm's average variable cost, the firm will find it advantageous to _____ in the short run. To understand this keep in mind a simple rule: a firm will shut down when it _____ more by operating than it loses by shutting down.

29. _____   When the _____ is less than average variable costs, the firm's total revenues do not cover its variable costs:

$$P < AVC$$

$$P < \frac{VC}{Q}$$

$P \times Q < VC$	Profit = TR − TC
$TR < VC$	Profit = TR − (FC − VC)
	Profit = (TR − VC) − FC

30. _____   By operating, the firm loses _____ than its fixed costs whenever price is less than average variable costs. On the other hand, if a firm shuts down, total revenues and variable

31. _____   costs are zero; the firm loses only its _____ costs. A firm will shut down whenever the price falls short of

32. _____   _____ variable cost.

PROFIT MAXIMIZATION AND MANAGERS' INCENTIVES

33. _____   In many firms those who _____ the firm's capital the are not the same individuals as those who manage operation of the firm. This is an example of the principle-agent phenomenon. The manager acts as an

34. _____   _____ for the owner. This separation of ownership and management creates a conflict: The owner is concerned

35. _____   with the firm's _____, while the manager is concerned with benefits. The manager (who is not the sole

36. _____   owner) will operate the firm to produce _____ profit and more benefits than the owner would like. Management contracts lessen this conflict. These contracts provide

37. _____   _____ with incentives to encourage profit-maximizing behavior. The contracts represent a compromise. Profits will be greater than in the pure agent case, but less than the owner-operated case.

MULTIPLE-CHOICE QUESTIONS

38. _____ Economists typically assume that firms
   a. maximize sales.
   b. maximize revenues.
   c. maximize profits.
   d. maximize costs.
   e. are completely unpredictable.

39. _____ A firm's total revenue equals
   a. price times the quantity it sells.
   b. price times its average cost.
   c. average cost times the quantity it sells.
   d. marginal cost times the quantity it sells.
   e. a and c.

40. _____ To maximize profits, a firm produces the level of output at which its
   a. marginal revenue equals price.
   b. average cost is minimized.
   c. marginal revenue equals its marginal cost.
   d. average cost equals the price.
   e. c and d.

41. _____ A firm's marginal cost equals
   a. the additional revenue the firm obtains from the sale of one additional unit of output.
   b. total costs divided by output.
   c. the ratio of total costs to output.
   d. the additional costs the firm incurs from the production of one additional unit of output.
   e. the additional profits the firm obtains from the production and sale of one additional unit of output.

42. _____ A firm's marginal revenue equals
   a. the additional revenue the firm obtains from the sale of one additional unit of output.
   b. total revenue divided by output.
   c. the ratio of total revenue to output.
   d. the additional costs the firm incurs from the production of one additional unit of output.
   e. the additional profits the firm obtains from the production and sale of one additional unit of output.

43. _____ If a firm's marginal revenue exceeds its marginal cost, additional production will
    a. decrease its costs.
    b. increase its revenues by more than its costs.
    c. increase its costs by more than its revenues.
    d. decrease its profits.
    e. a and b.

44. _____ If a firm's marginal cost exceeds it marginal revenue, additional production will
    a. decrease its costs.
    b. increase its revenues by more than its costs.
    c. increase its costs by more than its revenues.
    d. increase its profits.
    e. b and d.

45. _____ If a firm is a price taker,
    a. its output decisions will not affect the price.
    b. additional production by the firm will lower the price.
    c. its marginal revenue will equal the price.
    d. its marginal revenue will be less than the price.
    e. a and c.

46. _____ If price falls whenever the firm increases production, marginal revenue will
    a. equal the initial price.
    b. equal the new price.
    c. be less than the price.
    d. be greater than the new price.
    e. a and d.

47. _____ A good's price elasticity of demand reflects how sensitive the quantity demanded is to a change in
    a. the price of the good in question.
    b. income.
    c. the price of another good.
    d. consumer preferences.
    e. b and c.

48. _____ The price elasticity of demand equals
   a. the change in the quantity demanded caused by a one unit (1 dollar) change in price.
   b. the percent change in the quantity demanded caused by a 1 percent change in income.
   c. the ratio of the change in the quantity demanded to the change in the price.
   d. the ratio of the percent change in the quantity demanded to the percent change in the price.
   e. a and c.

49. _____ If a firm faces an inelastic demand curve for the good it produces, then the firm's marginal revenue
   a. must be negative.
   b. must be positive.
   c. must be zero.
   d. may be positive, negative, or zero.
   e. is never negative.

50. _____ If a firm faces an elastic demand curve for the good it produces, then the firm's marginal revenue
   a. must be negative.
   b. must be positive.
   c. must be zero.
   d. may be positive, negative, or zero.
   e. equals −1.

51. _____ Most economists support the use of the profit maximization hypothesis because
   a. most firm managers rank profits as their only goal when they are polled.
   b. the hypothesis has proven to be an accurate predictor of firm behavior in the real world.
   c. of the survivorship principle.
   d. no other hypothesis has been advanced.
   e. b and c.

52. _____ A profit-maximizing firm in a perfectly competitive industry will at all times produce the level of output at which price equals its
   a. average cost regardless of the relationship between price and average variable cost.
   b. average cost as long as price exceeds average variable cost.
   c. marginal cost regardless of the relationship between price and average variable cost.
   d. marginal cost as long as price exceeds average variable cost.
   e. a and d.

53. _____ An individual firm's supply curve is its
   a. marginal cost curve.
   b. marginal cost curve as long as price exceeds average variable cost.
   c. average cost curve.
   d. average cost curve as long as price exceeds average variable cost.
   e. a and c.

54. _____ If a firm were to operate when the price is less than its average variable cost,
   a. variable costs would exceed total revenues.
   b. total costs would exceed total revenues.
   c. losses would be less than fixed costs.
   d. losses would be greater than fixed costs.
   e. a, b, and d.

55. _____ In the short run, whenever the price is less than average variable cost, the firm will
   a. shut down.
   b. exit the industry.
   c. expand production.
   d. continue to operate.
   e. c and d.

56. _____ When the ownership and management of a firm are separated,
   a. the owner acts as the manager's agent.
   b. the owner and manager typically have identical interests.
   c. the owner and manager typically have different interests.
   d. a and b.
   e. a and c.

RUNNING GLOSSARY

57. _____ _____ revenue: the extra revenue a firm receives when it sells one more unit of output.

58. _____ _____ Price taker: a firm or individual whose decisions regarding buying or selling have no effect on the prevailing market _____ of a good or service.

59. _____ Revenue maximization: a goal for firms in which they work to maximize their total _____ rather than profits.

60. _____ _____ pricing: determining the selling price of a good by adding a percentage to the average cost of producing it.

61. _____ Shutdown price: the price below which the firm will choose to produce no output in the _____ run. Equal to
62. _____ minimum average _____ cost.

63. _____ _____: the role of making economic decisions for another party; for example, the manager of a firm being hired to act for the owner.

ANSWERS

1. quantity	22. revenue	43. b
2. revenue	23. profit	44. c
3. cost	24. equals	45. e
4. equals	25. price	46. c
5. exceeds	26. price	47. a
6. rise	27. shut down	48. d
7. equal	28. loses	49. a
8. taker	29. price	50. b
9. equals	30. more	51. e
10. equal	31. fixed	52. d
11. less	32. average	53. b
12. revenue	33. own	54. e
13. price	34. agent	55. a
14. increase	35. profits	56. c
15. fall	36. less	57. Marginal
16. negative	37. managers	58. price
17. positive	38. c	59. revenue
18. average	39. a	60. Markup
19. fall	40. c	61. short
20. less	41. d	62. variable
21. beneath	42. a	63. Agent

PART 3

PRODUCTION, COSTS, AND SUPPLY

WALKING TOUR PROBLEMS

COST MINIMIZATION

1. The wage rate of labor is $20.00 and the rental rate of capital is $10.00. The firm's rate of technical substitution is 1.0.

    a. What is the wage-rental ratio; that is, what is the wage rate divided by the rental rate?

       The wage rate is $20.00 and the rental rate is $10. The wage-rental ratio is _____.

1. _____

       The answer is 2.0.

    b. Can the firm reduce costs without decreasing its level of output? Should the firm use more, less, or the same amount of labor?

       Since the wage-rental ratio does not equal the rate of technical substitution, the firm _____ reduce its costs without producing less output.

2. _____

       The answer is yes.

       The firm's rate of technical substitution is 1.0; if the firm uses 1 less unit of labor, _____ additional unit of capital is required to keep the level of production constant. The wage-rental ratio is 2.0; if the firm hires 1 less unit of labor, _____ additional units of capital can be hired while keeping its total costs constant. Consequently, if the firm hires 1 less unit of labor and 1 additional unit of capital, production will remain the same and total costs will _____.

3. _____

4. _____

5. _____

The answer is hire less labor and more capital.

2. The wage rate of labor is $30.00 and the rental rate of capital is $10.00. The firm's rate of technical substitution is 4.0.

   a. What is the wage-rental ratio; that is, what is the wage rate divided by the rental rate?

   6. _____

   The wage rate is $30.00 and the rental rate is $10. The wage-rental ratio is _____.

   The answer is 3.0.

   b. Can the firm reduce costs without decreasing its level of output? Should the firm use more, less, or the same amount of labor?

   7. _____

   Since the wage-rental ratio does not equal the rate of technical substitution, the firm can reduce its costs _____ producing less output.

   The answer is yes.

   8. _____
   9. _____

   The firm's rate of technical substitution is 4.0; if the firm uses 1 more unit of labor, 4 fewer units of capital can be used while keeping the level of production _____. The wage-rental ratio is 3.0; if the firm hires 1 more unit of labor, _____ fewer units of capital must be hired to keep its total costs constant. Consequently, if the firm hires 1 more unit of labor and 4 fewer units of capital, production will

   10. _____

   remain the same and total costs will _____.

   The answer is hire more labor and less capital.

3. The wage rate of labor is $20.00 and the rental rate of capital is $10.00. The firm's rate of technical substitution is 2.0.

   a. What is the wage-rental ratio; that is, what is the wage rate divided by the rental rate?

   11. _____

12. _____

13. _____

       b. Can the firm reduce costs without decreasing its level of output? Should the firm use more, less, or the same amount of labor?

4. The wage rate of labor is $5.00 and the rental rate of capital is $10.00. The firm's rate of technical substitution is 0.8.

       a. What is the wage-rental ratio; that is, what is the wage rate divided by the rental rate?

14. _____

       b. Can the firm reduce costs without decreasing its level of output? Should the firm use more, less, or the same amount of labor?

15. _____

16. _____

5. The wage rate of labor is $20.00 and the rental rate of capital is $10.00. The firm's rate of technical substitution is 0.5.

       a. What is the wage-rental ratio; that is, what is the wage rate divided by the rental rate?

17. _____

       b. Can the firm reduce costs without decreasing its level of output? Should the firm use more, less, or the same amount of labor?

18. _____

19. _____

PROFIT MAXIMIZATION AND SHUTDOWN

1. The price is $.60. A firm is producing 100 units of output; its marginal revenue is $.60, its marginal cost is $.50, its average cost is $.65, and its average variable cost is $.30.

       a. Is the firm operating in a perfectly competitive industry?

20. _____

21. _____

In a perfectly competitive industry firms are price _____; a firm's marginal revenue equals the _____. Since both the price and marginal revenue are $.60, the industry is perfectly competitive.

The answer is yes.

b. Is the firm maximizing its profits? Should the firm produce more, less, or the same amount of output?

To determine whether a firm is maximizing its profits, compare its marginal revenue with its

22. _____

23. _____

_____. Since marginal revenue exceeds marginal cost, profits _____ being maximized.

The answer is no.

24. _____

The production and sale of one additional unit of output will increase total revenues by $_____ (marginal revenue) and increase total costs by $.50

25. _____

(_____); profits increase when the additional unit is produced.

The answer is produce more.

c. What is the firm's total revenue?

26. _____

Total revenue equals _____ times quantity. The price is $.60 and the quantity is 100; total revenue

27. _____

equals $_____.

The answer is $60.00.

d. What is the firm's total cost?

28. _____

Total cost equals _____ cost times quantity. Average cost is $.65 and the quantity is 100; total cost

29. _____

equals $_____.

The answer is $65.00.

e. Are the firm's profits currently positive, negative, or zero?

The most straightforward way of answering this question is to calculate profits. Profits equal the

30. _____

_____ between the firm's total revenue and total cost: $60.00 less $65.00, that is negative

31. _____

$_____. Another way to determine the sign of

32. _____

33. _____

34. _____

35. _____

36. _____

37. _____

the firm's profits is to compare price and _____ cost. Total revenue equals price times _____. Total cost equals average cost times _____. Consequently if price exceeds average cost, profit is _____; if average cost exceeds price, profit is negative; if price equals average cost, profit is _____. Since average cost is $.65 and price is $.60, profits are currently _____.

The answer is negative.

f. Would it be advantageous for the firm to shut down rather than to continue its current mode of operation?

38. _____

39. _____

40. _____

41. _____

42. _____

43. _____

To determine whether or not a firm should shut down compare _____ and average variable cost. Total cost equals the sum of fixed and variable cost. Whenever average variable cost exceeds _____, variable cost (which equals average variable cost times quantity) exceeds total revenue (which equals price times quantity) and the firm incurs a loss that _____ its fixed cost; consequently, whenever average variable cost exceeds price, it is advantageous for the firm to _____ thereby incurring a loss just equal to its fixed cost. On the other hand, whenever price _____ average variable costs, it is advantageous for the firm to continue to operate. Since price is $.60 and average variable cost is $.30, the firm will _____ to operate.

The answer is no.

2. The price is $.80. A firm is producing 200 units of output; its marginal revenue is $.80, its marginal cost is $.80, its average cost is $1.25, and its average variable cost is $.90.

a. Is the firm operating in a perfectly competitive industry?

44. _____

45. _____

In a perfectly competitive industry firms are price _____; a firm's marginal revenue equals the _____. Since both the price and marginal

- 129 -

revenue are $.80, the industry is perfectly competitive.

The answer is yes.

b. Is the firm maximizing its profits? Should the firm produce more, less, or the same amount of output?

46. _____

47. _____

To determine whether a firm is maximizing its profits, compare its marginal _____ with its marginal cost. Since marginal revenue equals marginal cost, profits _____ being maximized.

The answer is yes.

c. What is the firm's total revenue?

48. _____

49. _____

Total revenue equals _____ times quantity. The price is $.80 and the quantity is 200; total revenue equals $_____.

The answer is $160.00.

d. What is the firm's total cost?

50. _____

51. _____

Total cost equals _____ cost times quantity. Average cost is $1.25 and the quantity is 200; total cost equals $_____.

The answer is $250.00.

e. Are the firm's profits currently positive, negative, or zero?

52. _____

53. _____
54. _____

55. _____
56. _____
57. _____

The most straightforward way of answering this question is to calculate profits. Profits equal the difference between the firm's total _____ and total cost: $160.00 less $250.00, that is negative $_____. Another way to determine the sign of the firm's profits is to compare _____ and average cost. Total revenue equals _____ times quantity. Total cost equals _____ cost times quantity. Consequently if price _____ average cost,

- 130 -

58. _____

profit is positive; if average cost _____ price, profit is negative; if price equals average cost, profit is zero. Since average cost is $1.25 and price is $.80, profits are currently negative.

The answer is negative.

f. Would it be advantageous for the firm to shut down rather than to continue its current mode of operation?

59. _____

60. _____

61. _____

To determine whether or not a firm should shut down compare _____ and average variable cost. Total costs equal the sum of fixed and variable cost. Whenever average variable cost _____ price, variable cost (which equals average variable cost times quantity) exceeds total revenue (which equals price times quantity) and the firm incurs a loss that _____ its fixed cost; consequently, whenever average variable cost exceeds price, it is advantageous for the firm to shut down thereby incurring a loss just equal to its fixed cost. On the other hand, whenever price exceeds average variable costs it is advantageous for the firm to continue to operate. Since price is $.80 and average variable cost is $.90, it is advantageous for the firm to

62. _____

_____.

The answer is yes.

3. The price is $1.10. A firm is producing 1,000 units of output; its marginal revenue is $.90, its marginal cost is $1.00, its average cost is $1.05, and its average variable cost is $.60.

63. _____
64. _____

a. Is the firm maximizing its profits? Should the firm produce more, less, or the same amount of output?

65. _____

b. What is the firm's total revenue?

66. _____

c. What is the firm's total cost?

67. _____

d. Are the firm's profits currently positive, negative, or zero?

- 131 -

68. _____

  e. Would it be advantageous for the firm to shut down or to continue its current mode of operation?

 4. The price is $2.00. A firm is producing 500 units of output; its marginal revenue is $2.00, its marginal cost is $2.00, its average cost is $1.50, and its average variable cost is $.90.

69. _____
70. _____

  a. Is the firm maximizing its profits? Should the firm produce more, less, or the same amount of output?

71. _____

  b. What is the firm's total revenue?

72. _____

  c. What is the firm's total cost?

73. _____

  d. Are the firm's profits currently positive, negative, or zero?

74. _____

  e. Would it be advantageous for the firm to shut down or to continue its current mode of operation?

 5. The price is $1.50. A firm is producing 1,000 units of output; its marginal revenue is $.90, its marginal cost is $.80, its average cost is $1.80, and its average variable cost is $1.40.

75. _____
76. _____

  a. Is the firm maximizing its profits? Should the firm produce more, less, or the same amount of output?

77. _____

  b. What is the firm's total revenue?

78. _____

  c. What is the firm's total cost?

79. _____

  d. Are the firm's profits currently positive, negative, or zero?

80. _____

  e. Would it be advantageous for the firm to shut down or to continue its current mode of operation?

ANSWERS

1. 2.0
2. can
3. 1
4. 2
5. decrease
6. 3.0
7. without
8. constant
9. 3
10. decrease
11. 2.0
12. No
13. The same amount
14. 0.5
15. Yes
16. More labor
17. 2.0
18. Yes
19. More labor
20. takers
21. price
22. marginal cost
23. are not
24. .60
25. marginal cost
26. price
27. 60.00

28. average
29. 65.00
30. difference
31. 5.00
32. average
33. quantity
34. quantity
35. positive
36. zero
37. negative
38. price
39. price
40. exceeds
41. shut down
42. exceeds
43. continue
44. takers
45. price
46. revenue
47. are
48. price
49. 160.00
50. average
51. 250.00
52. revenue
53. 90.00
54. price

55. price
56. average
57. exceeds
58. exceeds
59. price
60. exceeds
61. exceeds
62. shut down
63. No
64. Produce less
65. $1,100.00
66. $1,050.00
67. Positive
68. Continue to operate
69. Yes
70. The same amount
71. $1,000.00
72. $750.00
73. Positive
74. Continue to operate
75. No
76. Produce more
77. $1,500.00
78. $1,800.00
79. Negative
80. Continue to operate

PART 4

MODELS OF MARKET EQUILIBRIUM

CHAPTER 8

THE PERFECTLY COMPETITIVE MODEL

LEARNING OBJECTIVES
- The equilibrium price is the price at which the quantity demanded equals the quantity supplied.
- The short-run supply curve is the horizontal sum of each individual firm's supply curve.
- The short-run supply elasticity equals the percent change in quantity supplied in the short run resulting from a 1 percent change in the price.
- While firms cannot enter or exit an industry in the short run, they can in the long run.
- A long-run equilibrium requires every firm to earn zero economic profit; consequently, in the long run, price must equal minimum long-run average total cost.
- In a constant (decreasing) cost industry, the long-run supply curve is horizontal (upward sloping).

WALKING TOUR SUMMARIES

PRICING IN THE VERY SHORT RUN

1. _____ In the very short run, there is _____ supply response; the quantity supplied is fixed. Firms do not have time to adjust their production levels; they will supply the same quantity of goods regardless of the price. In the very short
2. _____ run the supply curve is _____.

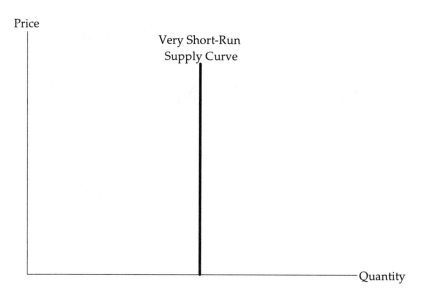

Figure 8.1: *Very Short-Run Supply Curve*

SHORT-RUN SUPPLY

3. _____   In the short run, the number of firms in an industry is _____ _____; that is, firms can neither exit nor enter the industry. Each firm can adjust its production level by

4. _____ varying some (but not all) of its _____, however.

5. _____ The firm's short-run supply curve is its _____ cost curve (as long as price exceeds average variable cost):

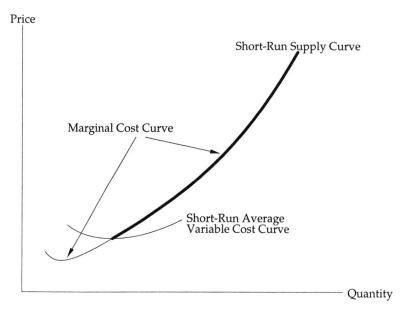

Figure 8.2: *A Firm's Short-Run Supply Curve*

6. _____ The _____ summation of each firm's individual short-run supply curve yields the upward sloping short-run market supply curve:

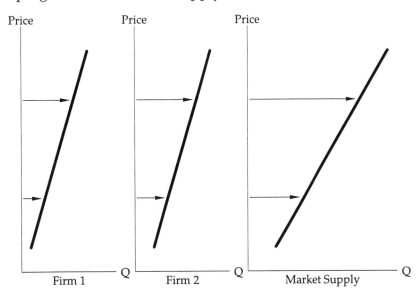

Figure 8.3: *The Market Short-Run Supply Curve*

SHORT-RUN PRICE DETERMINATION

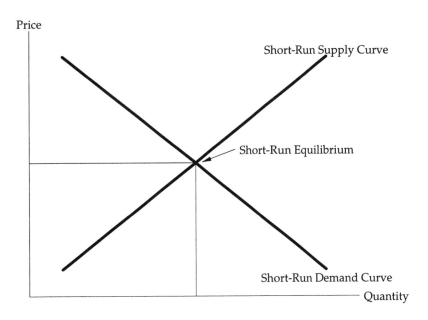

Figure 8.4: *Short-Run Market Equilibrium*

7. _____ The equilibrium is the price-quantity combination represented by the _____ of the market demand and

8. _____ _____ the quantity supplied. If the price were below the equilibrium level, a shortage would exist and market

9. _____ forces would push the price to _____. Alternatively, if the price were above the equilibrium, there would be

10. _____ _____ and the price would fall.

If a market that is initially in equilibrium experiences an increase in demand, the equilibrium will be

11. _____ destroyed. The quantity demanded will _____ the quantity supplied and the price will rise. In the very short run, the quantity supplied is fixed. The price rises until the

12. _____ quantity demanded _____ the fixed quantity supplied. That is, in the very short run the price adjusts so as to ration the fixed quantity supplied among those who demand the good. While firms cannot respond in the very short run, they are able to adjust their production levels in

13. _____ the _____ run. The short-run market supply curve is now relevant. A new equilibrium will be established where

14. _____ quantity demanded _____ the quantity supplied.

15. _____ The new equilibrium price will be _____ than the

16. _____ initial equilibrium price, but _____ than the price established in the very short run. The new equilibrium

17. _____ quantity _____ the initial equilibrium quantity.

supply curves. At the equilibrium the quantity demanded

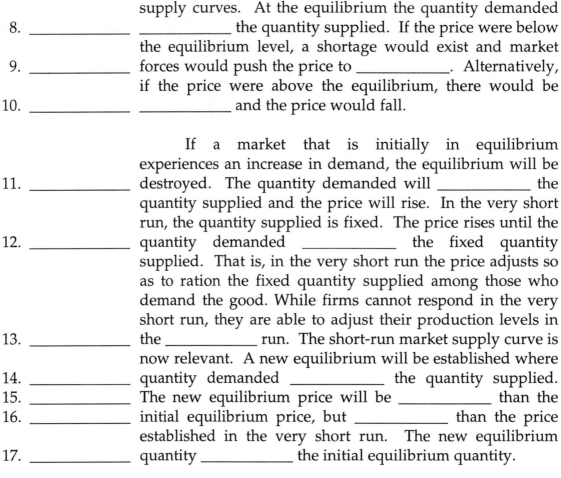

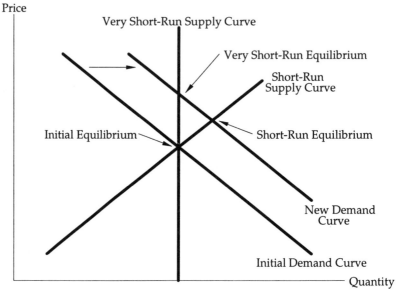

Figure 8.5: *Response to an Increase in Demand*

SHIFTS IN SUPPLY AND DEMAND CURVES

The demand curve for a good can shift only when something affecting demand changes other than the

18. _____ _____ of the good itself. When this happens
19. _____ economists say that a(n) _____ in demand occurs. A change in the price of a good itself will never cause the
20. _____ demand curve for that good to _____. A change in
21. _____ the price leads to a movement _____ the demand curve. Economists refer to a movement along a demand
22. _____ curve as a change in the _____ demanded.

23. _____ The _____ curve for a good can shift only when something affecting supply changes other than the price of the good itself. When this happens economists say that a change in supply occurs. A change in the
24. _____ _____ of a good itself will never cause the supply curve for that good to shift. A change in the price leads to a movement along the supply curve. Economists refer to a
25. _____ movement _____ a supply curve as a change in the quantity supplied.

SHORT-RUN SUPPLY ELASTICITY

The elasticity of supply indicates how sensitive the quantity
26. _____ supplied is to a change in the _____. More precisely, the elasticity of supply equals the percent change in the
27. _____ quantity supplied resulting from a 1 _____ change in the price:

$$\text{Supply Elasticity} = \frac{\text{Percent Change in Quantity Supplied}}{\text{Percent Change in Price}}$$

Whenever the quantity supplied is "very sensitive" to the
28. _____ price, economists say that supply is _____. More precisely, supply is elastic whenever a 1 percent change in price leads to a more than 1 percent change in quantity supplied. Alternatively, if the quantity supplied is "not very
29. _____ sensitive," supply is _____. Last, if a 1 percent
30. _____ change in the price leads to a(n) _____ percent change in quantity supplied, supply is unit elastic. In the
31. _____ very short run, supply is completely _____ because the quantity supplied cannot change; consequently, the quantity supplied is completely insensitive to the price. In

32. _____ the short run, supply can be elastic, inelastic, or unit elastic because the quantity supplied _____ whenever the price increases.

SHIFTS IN DEMAND AND SUPPLY CURVES AND THE IMPORTANCE OF ELASTICITIES

33. _____ For a given shift of the supply curve, the equilibrium price will change less and less (and the equilibrium quantity changes more and more) as demand elasticity _____.

34. _____ For a given shift of the demand curve, the equilibrium price will change less and less (and the equilibrium quantity changes more and more) as supply elasticity _____.

THE LONG RUN

35. _____ In the long run, supply responses are _____ flexible than in the short run for two reasons. First, firms can

36. _____ _____ all inputs in the long run, while in the short run firms can adjust only variable inputs. Second, firms

37. _____ can _____ or exit an industry in the long run in response to profit opportunities.

A long-run equilibrium differs from a short-run equilibrium in two ways. First, firms must be maximizing their profits with respect to all inputs. This means that marginal revenue (which equals price in a perfectly

38. _____ competitive market) must equal long-run _____ cost. Second, firms must have no incentive to enter or leave the industry. This condition is met whenever economic profits

39. _____ equal _____. If economic profits are negative, firms
40. _____ have an incentive to _____ the industry; positive profits cause firms to enter.

Economic profits are zero whenever price equals

41. _____ _____ cost. To understand why, recall that total revenues equal price times quantity and observe that total costs equal average cost times quantity:

$$
\begin{aligned}
\text{Profits} &= \text{TR} - \text{TC} \\
&= P \times Q - AC \times Q \\
&= (P - AC) \times Q
\end{aligned}
$$

42. _____ Profits will be _____ whenever price equals average cost. In summary, a long-run equilibrium in a perfectly competitive market requires both marginal cost and average cost to equal the price:

$$P = MC = AC$$

43. _____ Furthermore, recall that the marginal cost and average cost curves intersect at _____ average cost; consequently, price will equal minimum average cost when a(n)
44. _____ _____-run equilibrium is achieved.

LONG-RUN SUPPLY CURVE

45. _____ The long-run supply curve represents all the price-quantity combinations that are _____-run equilibria. To find one point on the long-run supply curve, first choose a level of demand; in a graph, choose a demand curve. With the short-run supply curve you can now determine the current equilibrium. At this equilibrium, does the price equal average cost? If so, you have found one point on the long-run supply curve. If not, changes will occur in the long
46. _____ run. Suppose that price exceeds _____ cost; profits
47. _____ are positive which leads to _____ in the long run.
48. _____ Entry shifts the short-run supply curve to the _____
49. _____ causing the price to _____. Entry continues until price equals average cost at which time you have now found one point of the long-run supply curve. By considering all possible positions of the demand curve, we can construct the long-run supply curve by following this procedure.

50. _____ If the industry is a(n) _____ cost industry, the entry of new firms does not affect the cost of existing firms
51. _____ and the long-run supply curve is _____. Alternatively, in an increasing cost industry, entry
52. _____ _____ the cost of existing firms and the long-run
53. _____ supply curve is _____ sloping. Last, the long-run
54. _____ supply curve is downward sloping in a(n) _____ cost industry.

55. _____ Supply is _____ elastic in the long run than in the short run. In the long run, firms can adjust production
56. _____ levels more easily because they can vary _____, not just some, inputs; therefore, each firm's level of production

57. _____ will be more sensitive to the _____. The possibility
of entry and exit also makes the quantity supplied
58. _____ _____ sensitive to the price.

MULTIPLE-CHOICE QUESTIONS

59. _____ In the very short run
   a. the quantity of output a firm produces is fixed.
   b. the quantity of output a firm produces can be changed.
   c. some (but not all) inputs the firm uses can be changed.
   d. all inputs the firm uses can be changed.
   e. b and c.

60. _____ In the short run
   a. the quantity of output a firm produces is fixed.
   b. the quantity of output a firm produces can be changed.
   c. some (but not all) inputs the firm uses can be changed.
   d. all inputs the firm uses can be changed.
   e. b and c.

61. _____ In the long run
   a. the quantity of output a firm produces can be changed.
   b. all inputs the firm uses can be changed.
   c. firms can enter or exit the industry.
   d. a and b.
   e. a, b, and c.

62. _____ In the short run the market supply curve is
   a. the horizontal sum of each firm's individual supply curve.
   b. the horizontal sum of each firm's average cost curve.
   c. the horizontal sum of each firm's average cost curve as long as price exceeds average variable cost.
   d. the horizontal sum of each firm's marginal cost curve as long as price is less than average variable cost.
   e. a and d.

63. _____ If the (actual) price exceeds the equilibrium price, market forces tend to make the
    a. price increase until it equals the equilibrium price.
    b. price decrease until it equals the equilibrium price.
    c. equilibrium price increase until it equals the price.
    d. equilibrium price decrease until it equals the price.
    e. b and c.

64. _____ In the very short run an increase in demand will lead to
    a. an increase in price and an increase in quantity.
    b. an increase in price and a decrease in quantity.
    c. an increase in price and no change in quantity.
    d. a decrease in price and an increase in quantity.
    e. a decrease in price and a decrease in quantity.

65. _____ In the short run an increase in demand will lead to
    a. an increase in price and an increase in quantity.
    b. an increase in price and a decrease in quantity.
    c. an increase in price and no change in quantity.
    d. a decrease in price and an increase in quantity.
    e. a decrease in price and a decrease in quantity.

66. _____ A good's elasticity of supply indicates how sensitive the quantity supplied is to a change in
    a. the price of the good in question.
    b. income.
    c. price of another good.
    d. consumer preferences.
    e. a and b.

67. _____ The elasticity of supply equals
    a. the change in the quantity supplied caused by a 1 unit (1 dollar) change in price.
    b. the percent change in the quantity supplied caused by a 1 percent change in price.
    c. the ratio of the change in the quantity supplied to the change in the price.
    d. the ratio of the percent change in the price to the percent change in the quantity demanded supplied.
    e. b and d.

68. _____ Whenever the elasticity of supply exceeds 1, supply is said to be
   a. elastic.
   b. unit elastic.
   c. inelastic, but not completely inelastic.
   d. completely inelastic.
   e. normal.

69. _____ Whenever the elasticity of supply equals 1, supply is said to be
   a. elastic.
   b. unit elastic.
   c. inelastic, but not completely inelastic.
   d. completely inelastic.
   e. normal.

70. _____ Whenever the elasticity of supply is between 0 and 1, supply is said to be
   a. elastic.
   b. unit elastic.
   c. inelastic, but not completely inelastic.
   d. completely inelastic.
   e. normal.

71. _____ Whenever the elasticity of supply equals 0, supply is said to be
   a. elastic.
   b. unit elastic.
   c. inelastic, but not completely inelastic.
   d. completely inelastic.
   e. normal.

72. _____ In the very short run, the elasticity of supply
   a. is elastic.
   b. is unit elastic.
   c. is inelastic, but not completely inelastic.
   d. is completely inelastic.
   e. may be elastic, inelastic, or unit elastic.

73. _____ In the short run, a firm's economic profits
   a. must be positive.
   b. must be negative.
   c. must be zero.
   d. may be positive, negative, or zero.
   e. cannot be zero.

74. _____ In long-run equilibrium, a firm's economic profits
   a. must be positive.
   b. must be negative.
   c. must be zero.
   d. may be positive, negative, or zero.
   e. cannot be zero.

75. _____ A firm's profits must be positive whenever the price is
   a. greater than marginal cost.
   b. greater than average cost.
   c. greater than average variable cost.
   d. less than marginal cost.
   e. less than average cost.

76. _____ A firm's profits must be negative whenever the price is
   a. greater than marginal cost.
   b. greater than average cost.
   c. greater than average variable cost.
   d. less than marginal cost.
   e. less than average cost.

77. _____ The long-run supply curve
   a. represents all the price-quantity combinations that are long-run equilibria.
   b. is the vertical sum of each firm's average cost curve.
   c. is the vertical sum of each firm's marginal cost curve.
   d. is the horizontal sum of each firm's average cost curve.
   e. is the horizontal sum of each firm's marginal cost curve.

78. _____ In a constant cost industry, the entry of new firms
   a. increases the costs of firms already in the industry.
   b. decreases the costs of firms already in the industry.
   c. has no effect on the costs of firms already in the industry.
   d. may increase, decrease, or have no effect on the costs of firms already in the industry.
   e. none of the above.

79. _____ In an increasing cost industry, the entry of new firms
   a. increases the costs of firms already in the industry.
   b. decreases the costs of firms already in the industry.
   c. has no effect on the costs of firms already in the industry.
   d. may increase, decrease, or have no effect on the costs of firms already in the industry.
   e. none of the above.

80. _____ In a constant cost industry, the long-run supply curve
        a. is upward sloping.
        b. is downward sloping.
        c. is horizontal.
        d. is U-shaped.
        e. may have any shape.

81. _____ In an increasing cost industry, the long-run supply curve
        a. is upward sloping.
        b. is downward sloping.
        c. is horizontal.
        d. is U-shaped.
        e. may have any shape.

RUNNING GLOSSARY

82. _____ Supply response: the change in quantity of output in response to a change in _____ conditions.

83. _____ Market period: a short period of time during which quantity supplied is _____.

84. _____ Equilibrium price: the price at which the quantity demanded by buyers of a good is equal to the quantity _____ of the good by sellers.

85. _____ _____ supply curve: the relationship between market price and quantity supplied of a good in the short run.

86. _____ External price effects: effects that changes in the level of production of an industry have on the prices of _____ to that industry.

87. _____ Short-run elasticity of supply: the percent change in quantity supplied in the short run in response to a(n) _____ percent change in price.

88. _____ _____ cost industry: an industry in which entry or exit of firms has no effect on the cost curves of the firms in the industry.

89. _____ Tax incidence theory: the study of the final burden of a tax after considering all market _____ to it.

90. _____ Increasing cost industry: an industry in which the entry of firms _____ the costs of the firms in the industry.

91. _____ Long-run elasticity of supply: the percent change in quantity _____ in the long run in response to a 1 percent change in price.

92. _____ Decreasing _____ industry: an industry in which the entry of firms decreases the costs of the firms in the industry.

ANSWERS

1. no	32. increases	63. b
2. vertical	33. increases	64. c
3. fixed	34. increases	65. a
4. inputs	35. more	66. a
5. marginal	36. change	67. b
6. horizontal	37. enter	68. a
7. intersection	38. marginal	69. b
8. equals	39. zero	70. c
9. rise	40. exit	71. d
10. surplus	41. average	72. d
11. exceed	42. zero	73. d
12. equals	43. minimum	74. c
13. short	44. long	75. b
14. equals	45. long	76. e
15. higher	46. average	77. a
16. lower	47. entry	78. c
17. exceeds	48. right	79. a
18. price	49. fall	80. c
19. change	50. constant	81. a
20. shift	51. horizontal	82. demand
21. along	52. increases	83. fixed
22. quantity	53. upward	84. supplied
23. supply	54. decreasing	85. Short-run
24. price	55. more	86. inputs
25. along	56. all	87. 1
26. price	57. price	88. Constant
27. percent	58. more	80. reactions
28. elastic	59. a	90. increases
29. inelastic	60. e	91. supplied
30. 1	61. e	92. cost
31. inelastic	62. a	

CHAPTER 9

APPLYING THE COMPETITIVE MODEL

LEARNING OBJECTIVES
- Consumer surplus equals the total value individuals place upon the consumption of the good less the amount consumers must pay for it.
- Geometrically, consumer surplus equals the area beneath the demand curve that lies above the price.
- Producer surplus equals the total revenue firms receive from the sale of the good less the opportunity cost incurred from producing the good.
- Geometrically, producer surplus equals the area above the supply curve that lies below the price.
- Deadweight loss refers to the losses of consumer and producer surplus that are not transferred to others.
- Price controls, taxes, and tariffs result in dead weight loss.

WALKING TOUR SUMMARIES

CONSUMER AND PRODUCER SURPLUS

1. _____ _____

2. _____

3. _____ _____

4. _____

Consumer surplus equals the total value that individuals receive from consuming a good, less what they _____ for the good at the current price, their total expenditures. Producer surplus equals the total value producers receive for a good, their total _____, less the opportunity costs they incur by producing the good. Geometrically, consumer surplus is the area beneath the _____ curve that lies above the price; producer surplus is the area above the supply curve that lies beneath the _____.

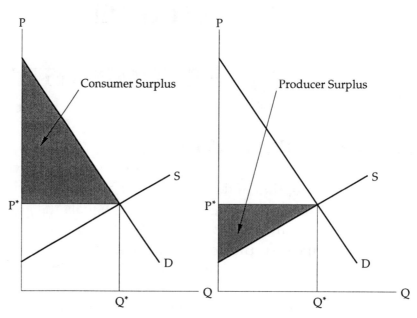

Figure 9.1: *Consumer Surplus and Producer Surplus*

5. _____ The short-run supply curve is the horizontal sum of each firm's _____ cost curve (as long as price exceeds average variable cost). Consequently, in the short run, producer surplus equals total revenues less variable costs; that is, producer surplus equals short-run profits plus

6. _____ short-run _____ costs.

7. _____ In the long-run equilibrium profits equal _____ and there are no fixed costs. The slope of the long-run supply curve depends on whether the firms in the industry experience increasing, constant, or decreasing costs. If the firms experience increasing costs, the long-run

8. _____ supply curve will be _____ sloping, reflecting the fact that the payments received by the firms' inputs

9. _____ _____ as output expands. In the long run, producer surplus equals the difference between the payments these inputs receive at the current price less the payments they would receive if the industry produced _____

10. _____ output.

PRICE CONTROLS AND SHORTAGES

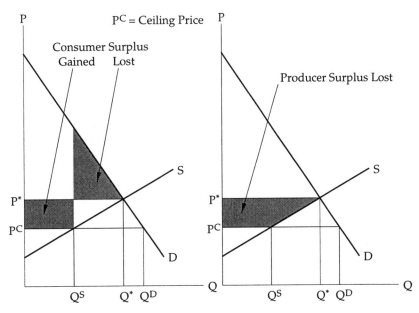

Figure 9.2: *Price Controls*

When the government imposes a price ceiling below the equilibrium price, both the consumers and the producers of the good are affected. Such a price ceiling creates a

11. _____ _____: The quantity demanded exceeds the quantity supplied. Some consumers are unable to buy as much of the good as they would like at the below-equilibrium price. Accordingly, some consumers are helped and some hurt. Those able to purchase the good at the below equilibrium

12. _____ price experience a(n) _____ in consumer surplus;

13. _____ those unable to purchase it experience a(n) _____ in consumer surplus. On the other hand, the producers

14. _____ experience an unambiguous _____ in producer

15. _____ surplus. In net, the losses _____ the gains; the price ceiling produces a welfare loss.

TAX INCIDENCE

The study of tax incidence recognizes that economic interactions can shift the burden of a tax from those legally obliged to pay it to others. A specific tax creates a wedge between what consumers pay and what firms get to keep. In particular, the price viewed from the standpoint of

16. _____ the consumers _____ the price as seen through the eyes of the firm by an amount just equal to the tax.

17. _____ Typically, the tax _____ the price as seen by the

18. _____ consumers, thereby _____ consumer surplus. The tax lowers the price as seen by the firms, thereby

19. _____ _____ producer surplus. The elasticities of demand and supply determine how the losses are distributed between individuals and firms. The relatively inelastic

20. _____ group will bear _____ of the burden. The combined loss in consumer and producer surplus exceeds the tax revenue raised; this difference is referred to as the

21. _____ _____ loss or excess burden of the tax.

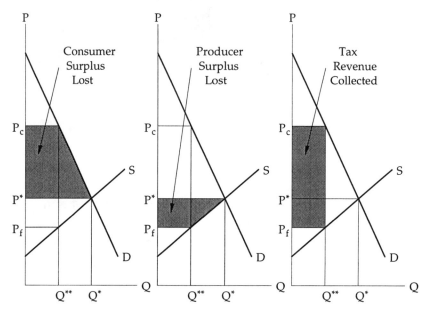

Figure 9.3: *Tax Incidence*

TRADE RESTRICTIONS

When a country opens its borders to the free trade of a good both consumers and producers are typically affected. In particular, if the world price is less than the domestic price, free trade would cause domestic production to

22. _____ _____ and domestic consumption to increase.

23. _____ Consumer surplus would _____ and producer surplus would decrease. In net, there is a welfare gain

24. _____ because the gain in consumer surplus _____ the loss in producer surplus.

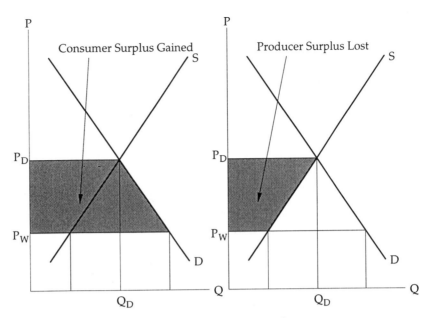

Figure 9.4: *Free Trade*

25. _____

26. _____

A tariff would have the effect of increasing the price within the country to a level _____ the world price. Starting at the free trade position, a tariff would reduce consumer surplus and increase producer surplus. There is a welfare loss, however, because the gain in producer surplus plus the revenue generated by the tariff falls short of the loss in _____surplus.

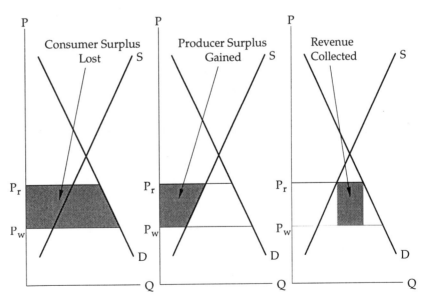

Figure 9.5: *Effect of a Tariff*

MULTIPLE-CHOICE QUESTIONS

27. _____ Consumer surplus equals
   a. the total value placed on the consumption of the good at its current price less what is actually paid for the good.
   b. what is actually paid for the good less the total value placed on the consumption of the good at its current price.
   c. the total revenue received for the good less the opportunity cost of producing the good.
   d. the opportunity cost of producing the good less the total revenue received for the good.
   e. none of the above.

28. _____ Producer surplus equals
   a. the total value placed on the consumption of the good at its current price less what is actually paid for the good.
   b. what is actually paid for the good less the total value placed on the consumption of the good at its current price.
   c. the total revenue received for the good less the opportunity cost of producing the good.
   d. the opportunity cost of producing the good less the total revenue received for the good.
   e. none of the above.

29. _____ Geometrically, consumer surplus equals the area beneath the
   a. demand curve and above the price.
   b. price and above the demand curve.
   c. supply curve and above the price.
   d. price and above the supply curve.
   e. demand curve.

30. _____ Geometrically, producer surplus equals the area beneath the
   a. demand curve and above the price.
   b. price and above the demand curve.
   c. supply curve and above the price.
   d. price and above the supply curve.
   e. supply curve.

31. _____ In the short run, producer surplus equals
   a. the difference between what the firms' inputs currently earn and what the inputs would earn if the industry produced nothing.
   b. zero.
   c. profits less fixed costs.
   d. profits plus fixed costs.
   e. a and d.

32. _____ In the long run, producer surplus equals
   a. the difference between what the firms' inputs currently earn and what the inputs would earn if the industry produced nothing.
   b. zero.
   c. profits less fixed costs.
   d. profits plus fixed costs.
   e. a and d.

33. _____ The imposition of a price ceiling below the equilibrium price
   a. increases producer surplus.
   b. decreases producer surplus.
   c. produces a welfare loss.
   d. b and c.
   e. has no effect.

34. _____ The imposition of a price ceiling above the equilibrium price
   a. increases producer surplus.
   b. decreases producer surplus.
   c. produces a welfare loss.
   d. b and c.
   e. has no effect.

35. _____ The imposition of a tax typically
   a. increases consumer surplus and increases producer surplus.
   b. increases consumer surplus and decreases producer surplus.
   c. decreases consumer surplus and increases producer surplus.
   d. decreases consumer surplus and decreases producer surplus.
   e. has no effect.

36. _____ The imposition of a tax on a good typically
    a. results in a deadweight loss.
    b. burdens those related to the production of the good.
    c. burdens those related to the consumption of the good.
    d. a, b, and, c.
    e. has no effect.

37. _____ Whenever the domestic price exceeds the world price, the opening of a country to free trade
    a. increases consumer surplus and increases producer surplus.
    b. increases consumer surplus and decreases producer surplus.
    c. decreases consumer surplus and increases producer surplus.
    d. decreases consumer surplus and decreases producer surplus.
    e. has no effect.

RUNNING GLOSSARY

38. _____ _____ surplus: the difference between the value individuals place upon the consumption of a good at its current price and what individuals actually pay for the good.

39. _____ Producer surplus: the difference between what firms actually _____ for the good and the opportunity cost of producing the good.

40. _____ Tax incidence: the study of how economic interactions _____ the burden of the tax from those legally obilged to pay it to others.

41. _____ _____ loss: losses in consumer and producer surplus that are not transferred to others.

42. _____ Tariff: a tax on a(n) _____ good.

ANSWERS

1. pay	15. exceed	29. a
2. revenue	16. exceeds	30. d
3. demand	17. raises	31. d
4. price	18. reducing	32. a
5. marginal	19. reducing	33. d
6. fixed	20. more	34. e
7. zero	21. deadweight	35. d
8. upward	22. decrease	36. d
9. increase	23. increase	37. b
10. no	24. exceeds	38. Consumer
11. shortage	25. above	39. receive
12. gain	26. consumer	40. shift
13. loss	27. a	41. Deadweight
14. loss	28. c	42. imported

CHAPTER 10

MONOPOLY

LEARNING OBJECTIVES

- Like the price taking firm, the profit-maximizing monopolist produces the level of output at which marginal revenue equals marginal cost.
- Unlike the price taking firm, marginal revenue is less than price for the monopolist.
- The price charged by a profit-maximizing monopolist exceeds marginal cost.
- The monopoly leads to a misallocation of resources; a deadweight loss results because price exceeds marginal cost.
- If a natural monopoly were regulated and forced to charge a price equal to marginal cost, deadweight loss would be eliminated; the monopoly would incur losses, however.

WALKING TOUR SUMMARIES

CAUSES OF MONOPOLY

1. _____

2. _____

3. _____

4. _____

Monopolies exist because other firms find it unprofitable or impossible to enter the market; barriers to _____ are the source of monopoly power. There are two types of barriers to entry: technical and legal. Technical barriers to entry exist whenever there is _____ average cost (increasing returns to scale) within the relevant range of production. In this case, one firm producing at high production levels has a distinct cost advantage over small firms producing low levels of output. Because average cost is _____ for the large firm, it could charge a price that would force the small, high-average-cost firms out of business. Ownership of low-cost methods of production, unique resources, unique management talents, etc. may also be a source of technical barriers to entry. Legal barriers to entry can exist due to patents, exclusive franchises, etc., which grant _____ firm unique rights.

PROFIT MAXIMIZATION

In one sense, a monopoly is just like a price taking firm: the monopolist's profit-maximizing production level occurs where marginal revenue _____ marginal cost. Monopolies differ from price taking firms in the relationship between marginal revenue and _____, however. Marginal revenue equals price for the price taking firm. Marginal revenue is _____ than price for the monopolist because the monopolist faces a downward sloping demand curve. When it sells one additional unit of output it must _____ the price on all units sold. While the sale of the additional unit itself tends to increase revenues by an amount equal to the price, the firm must sell all other units at the _____ price. In net, the change in total revenues from the sale of one additional unit (marginal revenue) will be _____ than the price. Let us now summarize. For a profit-maximizing monopolist:

$$P > MR = MC$$

_____ exceeds marginal cost for the profit-maximizing monopolist while price _____ marginal cost for the profit-maximizing price taking firm.

5. _____

6. _____

7. _____

8. _____

9. _____

10. _____

11. _____

12. _____

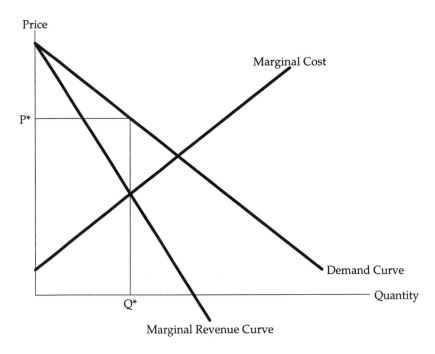

Figure 10.1: *Profit-Maximizing Monopolist*

MONOPOLY PROFITS

We calculate the profits of a monopoly just as we calculate the profits of any firm. A firm's profit equals total revenue less total cost, which in turn equals the quantity times the difference between price and _____ cost:

13. _____

$$\text{Profits} = \text{TR} - \text{TC}$$
$$= (P \times Q) - (AC \times Q)$$
$$= (P - AC) \times Q$$

In perfect competition, the existence of positive profits is a temporary phenomenon. In the long run, positive profits entice firms to enter the industry. The new firms drive profits to _____. The existence of barriers to entry in a monopoly means entry _____ occur. Accordingly, positive profits can persist in a monopoly.

14. _____
15. _____

WHAT'S WRONG WITH MONOPOLY?

Most people object to monopolies on distributional grounds. The owners of a monopoly (as opposed to the owners of a perfectly competitive firm) can receive _____ profits indefinitely. It is not true that these profits must be large, however. The size of profits depends on the difference between price and _____ cost. The existence of a monopoly does not guarantee that this difference will be large. In fact, the difference could even equal zero, meaning that the monopoly was earning zero profits.

16. _____

17. _____

A more sophisticated objection to monopoly concerns the allocation of resources. A profit-maximizing monopolist produces where price exceeds _____ cost. Consider an additional unit of output. The cost of producing the additional unit is _____ than what consumers are willing to pay for it. From a social perspective, the monopoly produces too _____ of the good. Society devotes too few resources to the production of the good.

18. _____

19. _____

20. _____

CONSUMER SURPLUS

If a monopoly could be a perfect price discriminator, it would be able to dole out the good one unit at a time. It would sell each unit to that consumer who would pay the

21. _____ _____ price. The perfect price discriminator could
22. _____ collect revenues equal to the area beneath the _____
23. _____ curve. This area represents the _____ value individuals place upon the consumption of the good. It is virtually impossible for a producer to practice perfect price discrimination, however; firms typically do not charge different prices to different buyers. Firms usually charge
24. _____ the _____ price to all. Most consumers buy the good
25. _____ at a price _____ that which the perfect price discriminator would charge. Economists call this bonus
26. _____ _____ surplus. Graphically, it is the area beneath
27. _____ the _____ curve which lies above the price. Consumer surplus equals the total value individuals place
28. _____ upon the consumption of the good _____ what they actually pay to purchase the good.

MONOPOLISTIC EFFECT ON ALLOCATION AND DISTRIBUTION

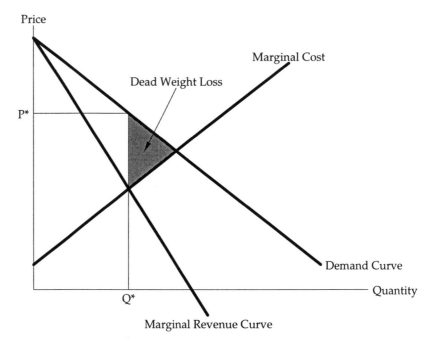

Figure 10.2: *Deadweight Loss of a Monopoly*

A monopoly restricts output below the competitive level. The restriction has two effects. Individuals have less of the "monopoly" good to consume. On the other hand,

29. _____ _____ inputs are used to produce the "monopoly" good; consequently, the inputs are used by other firms to produce "other" goods. The monopoly affects consumers in

30. _____ two ways: _____ of the "monopoly" good is

31. _____ produced, but _____ "other" goods are manufactured. The value consumers place upon the

32. _____ unproduced "monopoly" good _____ the value consumers place on the "other" goods, however. We call the

33. _____ difference the _____ loss of monopoly; it measures the distortion of resources caused by the monopoly. In addition to the allocation distortion, there is also a distributional effect. Part of what would be consumer

34. _____ surplus in a competitive situation becomes _____ for the monopolist.

PRICE DISCRIMINATION

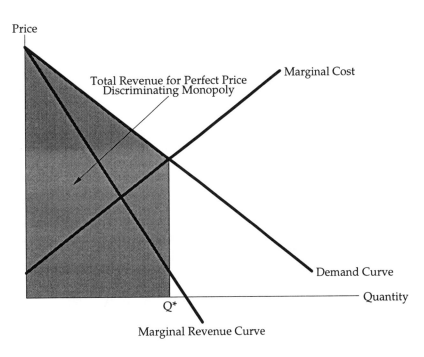

Figure 10.3: *Perfect Price Discriminating Monopolist*

In theory a monopoly could practice perfect price discrimination, selling each unit of output for the maximum amount that buyers are willing to pay. As the market demand curve suggests, the second unit would be sold for a slightly lower price than the first, the third unit for a slightly lower price than the second, etc. Total revenue would equal the area beneath the demand curve. The perfect price discriminating monopolist would continue to produce and

35. _____ sell output until the _____ of the last unit sold just equaled marginal cost. Paradoxically, a perfect price discrimination scheme would be efficient; deadweight loss would equal zero.

In practice, it is virtually impossible for a monopolist to be a perfect price discriminator. It is sometimes possible for a monopolist to divide its customers into several different groups, however. In this case, the monopolist could increase its profits by practicing price discrimination. That is, the monopolist could charge different groups different prices. To maximize profits, the monopolist charges the groups with the more inelastic

36. _____ demand a(n) _____ price.

REGULATION OF MONOPOLIES

To eliminate deadweight loss, monopolists must charge
37. _____ a price equal to _____ cost. Unfortunately, this
38. _____ cannot be done when a(n) _____ monopoly exists. Natural monopolies occur whenever average cost
39. _____ _____ in the relevant region of production. Since average cost is decreasing, marginal cost must be
40. _____ _____ than average cost. To eliminate deadweight loss entirely, the monopolist must be forced to charge a price
41. _____ _____ to marginal cost. Since marginal cost is less than average, forcing a natural monopoly to charge a price equal to marginal cost forces it to charge a price less than average cost. This means that the monopolist would incur a
42. _____ _____ and the firm would exit the industry in the
43. _____ _____ run. Economists have devised several approaches to resolve this dilemma, most notably
44. _____ _____-tier pricing and rate of return regulation.

- 164 -

PRICING FOR MULTI-PRODUCT MONOPOLIES

45. _____

46. _____

A firm that has pricing power in markets for two or more goods may find it advantageous to _____ the sale of the goods rather than sell each of the goods individually. Bundling may enable the firm to extract more of the _____ surplus from the buyers of the goods thereby increasing its profits.

MULTIPLE-CHOICE QUESTIONS

47. _____ Which of the following are referred to as technical barriers to entry?
    a. decreasing average cost
    b. patents
    c. increasing returns to scale
    d. a and c
    e. b and c

48. _____ Which of the following are referred to as legal barriers to entry?
    a. decreasing average cost
    b. patents
    c. increasing returns to scale
    d. a and c
    e. b and c

49. _____ A monopolist maximizes profits by producing the level of output at which
    a. marginal revenue equals marginal cost, just like the price taking firm.
    b. marginal revenue equals marginal cost, unlike the price taking firm.
    c. price equals marginal cost, just like the price taking firm.
    d. price equals marginal cost, unlike the price taking firm.
    e. price equals average cost.

50. _____ A monopolist's marginal revenue is
    a. equal to the price, just like the price taking firm.
    b. less than the price, just like the price taking firm.
    c. greater than the price, just like the price taking firm.
    d. equal to the price, unlike the price taking firm.
    e. less than the price, unlike the price taking firm.

51. _____ With a profit-maximizing monopolist, the price will be
   a. equal to marginal cost, just like the price taking firm.
   b. greater than marginal cost, just like the price taking firm.
   c. equal to marginal cost, unlike the price taking firm.
   d. less than marginal cost, unlike the price taking firm.
   e. greater than marginal cost, unlike the price taking firm.

52. _____ Monopolies earn positive profits
   a. in all cases.
   b. only when price exceeds marginal cost.
   c. only when price exceeds average cost.
   d. only when there are no barriers to entry.
   e. whenever price exceeds marginal cost.

53. _____ From a social perspective, a profit-maximizing monopoly typically
   a. produces too much output.
   b. produces too little output.
   c. produces the correct amount of output.
   d. uses too many resources.
   e. b and d.

54. _____ The area beneath the market demand curve represents the
   a. total value individuals place upon the consumption of the good.
   b. revenues that firms actually collect from the sale of the good.
   c. expenditures that households actually make to purchase the good.
   d. revenues a perfect price discriminator could collect from the sale of the good.
   e. a and d.

55. _____ In the real world, perfect price discrimination occurs
   a. in virtually every market.
   b. in virtually every monopolistic market.
   c. in about half the monopolistic markets.
   d. very infrequently, if ever.
   e. in virtually all competitive markets.

56. _____ A monopoly usually charges
   a. the same price to all customers.
   b. a different price to each customer.
   c. different prices to men and women.
   d. different prices to those with elastic and inelastic demand.
   e. c and d.

57. _____ Consumer surplus refers to the
   a. total value individuals place upon the consumption of the good.
   b. difference between the total value individuals place upon the consumption of the good and what individuals actually pay.
   c. expenditures individuals make to purchase the good.
   d. revenues a perfect price discriminator could collect from the sale of the good.
   e. a and d.

58. _____ Graphically, consumer surplus equals the area
   a. beneath the demand curve.
   b. between the demand curve and the price.
   c. beneath the marginal revenue curve.
   d. between the marginal revenue and marginal cost curves.
   e. b and d.

59. _____ The level of output produced by a profit-maximizing monopoly
   a. is below the competitive level.
   b. is above the competitive level.
   c. is equal to the competitive level.
   d. may be below, above, or equal to the competitive level.
   e. is never below the competitive level.

60. _____ The price charged by a profit-maximizing monopoly is
   a. below the competitive price.
   b. above the competitive price.
   c. equal to the competitive price.
   d. may be below, above, or equal to the competitive price.
   e. equal to marginal revenue.

61. _____ The deadweight loss of monopoly refers to the
    a. profits earned by the monopolist.
    b. profits earned by the monopolist in excess of what would be earned in the competitive case.
    c. value individuals place upon the goods that are not produced due to the monopolist's restriction of output.
    d. value of the inputs that are not used due to the monopolist's restriction of output.
    e. difference between c and d.

62. _____ To eliminate deadweight loss a monopoly must be forced to
    a. charge a price equal to marginal cost.
    b. charge a price equal to average cost.
    c. charge a price equal to average variable cost.
    d. reduce its level of production.
    e. a and d.

63. _____ Whenever a natural monopoly is forced to charge a price equal to marginal cost, the monopoly will
    a. incur a loss.
    b. earn a profit.
    c. cause no deadweight loss.
    d. wish to exit the industry in the long run.
    e. a, c, and d.

64. _____ When a profit-maximizing monopolist can divide its customers into separate groups, it will charge
    a. all groups the same price.
    b. groups with the more inelastic demand a higher price.
    c. groups with a more elastic demand a higher price.
    d. groups with unit elasticity the highest price.
    e. none of the above.

65. _____ When a profit-maximizing firm has pricing power in the markets for two or more of the goods it is producing, the firm
    a. should never bundle the sale of the goods; that is, the firm should sell each good as a separate entity.
    b. should always bundle the sale of the goods; that is, the firm should never sell a good as a separate entity.
    c. exert its pricing power only on one of the goods.
    d. may find it advantageous to bundle the sale of the goods.
    e. none of the above.

RUNNING GLOSSARY

66. _____ _____ to entry: factors that prevent new firms from entering a market or industry.

67. _____ _____ Natural monopoly: a firm that exhibits diminishing cost over a broad range of output levels.

68. _____ Monopoly rents: the _____ that a monopoly earns in the long run.

69. _____ Deadweight loss: a loss of consumer _____ that is not transferred to another economic actor.

70. _____ Price discrimination: the practice of charging _____ prices for a good in different markets.

71. _____ _____: the practice of selling two or more goods as a "package."

ANSWERS

1. entry	25. below	49. a
2. decreasing	26. consumer	50. e
3. less	27. demand	51. e
4. one	28. less	52. c
5. equals	29. fewer	53. b
6. price	30. less	54. e
7. less	31. more	55. d
8. lower	32. exceeds	56. a
9. lower	33. deadweight	57. b
10. less	34. profit	58. b
11. Price	35. price	59. a
12. equals	36. higher	60. b
13. average	37. marginal	61. e
14. zero	38. natural	62. a
15. cannot	39. decreases	63. e
16. positive	40. less	64. b
17. average	41. equal	65. d
18. marginal	42. loss	66. Barriers
19. less	43. long	67. average
20. little	44. two	68. profits
21. highest	45. bundle	69. surplus
22. demand	46. consumer	70. different
23. total	47. d	71. Bundling
24. same	48. b	

CHAPTER 11

IMPERFECT COMPETITION

LEARNING OBJECTIVES
- In the quasi-competitive model, each firm acts as a price taker.
- In a cartel model, each firm acts as a different division of a single monopoly firm thereby enabling the industry as a whole to maximize its profits.
- In a Cournot model, each firm assumes that the other firm's level of production is constant.
- Monopolistic competition refers to an industry in which each firm produces a differentiated product and entry is free; in the long run, firms will enter until economic profits are driven to zero.
- In a contestable market entry and exit are costless; therefore, in the long run profits must be zero.

WALKING TOUR SUMMARIES

PRICING OF HOMOGENEOUS GOODS

1. _____
2. _____
3. _____
4. _____
5. _____
6. _____
7. _____
8. _____
9. _____

There are _____ models that set outer limits on how an industry composed of a small number of firms (an oligopoly) may behave: the quasi-competitive and cartel models. In the quasi-competitive, model the firms behave like price _____. Each firm's marginal revenue equals the _____. Just as in the competitive case price will equal _____ cost. Furthermore, if there are no barriers to entry, price will also equal average cost in the _____ run. In the cartel model, the cartel acts as a multiplant _____ where firms behave as different divisions of a single large firm. As in the monopoly case, marginal revenue for the cartel will be _____ than price. When the cartel maximizes profits of the industry as a whole, price will _____ marginal cost. While it is in the firms' _____ interests to act like a cartel, three problems often limit their ability to do so. First, most cartels are illegal. Second, the implementation of a cartel agreement requires considerable information. Third, it is in

10. _____ the _____ interests of each firm to cheat on the cartel agreement.

OTHER PRICING POSSIBILITIES

11. _____ In addition to using the quasi-competitive and cartel models to illustrate the outer limits of _____ behavior, economists have developed many models that try to predict more precisely how oligopolies act. Perhaps the most famous two are the kinked demand and price leadership models. The kinked demand model hypothesizes that firms make decisions very cautiously. The model assumes that if one particular firm were to lower its

12. _____ price, other firms would react by _____ prices also.

13. _____ On the other hand, if one firm were to _____ its price, others would not respond. The kinked demand model explains why oligopolists rarely adjust their prices to

14. _____ changes in _____. The price leadership model hypothesizes that the firms in an oligopolistic industry look upon one firm (or a small group of firms) as the leader. Other firms will change their prices whenever the leader does.

THE COURNOT MODEL

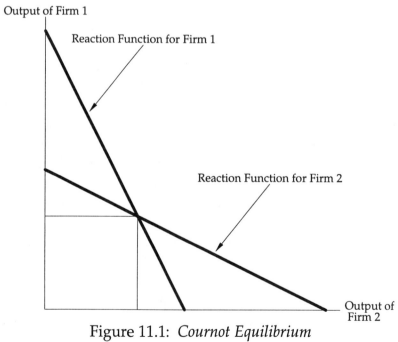

Figure 11.1: *Cournot Equilibrium*

The Cournot model describes the behavior of an industry composed of two firms, a(n) _____. Each firm assumes that the other firm's _____ will not change. Firm 1's reaction function describes its level of output _____ what firm 2 produces. Similarly, firm 2 has a reaction function that describes how much it will produce given firm 1's level of output. The intersection of the two reaction functions graphically represents a(n) _____ equilibrium. At a Cournot equilibrium each firm makes an _____ assumption about how much output the other is producing. The profits of the two firms are _____ than the level of profits in the monopoly case.

15. _____
16. _____
17. _____
18. _____
19. _____
20. _____

PRODUCT DIFFERENTIATION

The firms of many industries produce goods that are not homogeneous. In fact, firms often attempt to _____ their products in the minds of potential buyers. To differentiate their products firms engage in a wide variety of strategies. The decisions one firm makes will affect the decisions made by other firms in a very complicated way. Consequently, few general conclusions can be drawn in this case. The only conclusions we can make are rather obvious. Firms _____ price takers; furthermore, they often react to this very complex environment by using "rules of thumb."

21. _____
22. _____

ADVERTISING AND RESOURCE ALLOCATION

A pair of arguments suggest that our economy devotes too _____ resources to the production of advertising. The _____ product argument claims that firms will produce advertising until the change in total revenue resulting from one additional message equals the cost of the additional message. The additional revenue generated reflects individuals' willingness to pay for both the good itself and the information provided by the message. This means that the value consumers place on the information provided by the message must be _____ than the cost of providing the message. The second argument makes a distinction between constructive and combative advertising. Some argue that _____

23. _____
24. _____
25. _____
26. _____

advertising, advertising designed to draw customers from competitors rather than enlarge the market, is wasteful.

ENTRY BY NEW FIRMS

27. _____ If there are no barriers to entry, profits must equal _____ _____ in the long run. Positive profits will lure new firms into the industry driving the price down until price

28. _____ _____ average cost. In perfect competition, where all

29. _____ firms are price takers, the price will _____ minimum average cost. Alternatively, traditional analysis of

30. _____ oligopolies suggests that _____ will not equal minimum average cost when firms have some control over the price. Recently, some economists have challenged this view, however. The contestable markets hypothesis argues that potential entry will force firms to charge a price equal to minimum average cost. Otherwise, a "hit-and-run" entrant could earn a profit by producing at minimum average cost

31. _____ and charging a price slightly _____ than that which prevails. Note that if the contestable market view is correct and price equals minimum average cost, price will also

32. _____ equal _____ cost. The average cost and marginal

33. _____ cost curves intersect at _____ average cost.

MULTIPLE-CHOICE QUESTIONS

34. _____ Which of the following models sets outer limits on how an oligopoly producing homogeneous goods will behave?
   a. quasi-competitive model
   b. price leadership model
   c. cartel model
   d. a and c
   e. b and c

35. _____ In the quasi-competitive model,
   a. each firm behaves like a price taker.
   b. the firms behave like a multiplant monopoly where each firm acts like a separate division of a single monopolistic firm.
   c. the firms follow a price leader.
   d. each firm observes a kinked demand curve.
   e. c and d.

36. _____ In the quasi-competitive model, the price will
      a. equal marginal cost, just as in the perfectly competitive case.
      b. exceed marginal cost, just as in the perfectly competitive case.
      c. equal marginal cost, just as in the monopoly case.
      d. exceed marginal cost, just as in the monopoly case.
      e. equal average variable cost.

37. _____ In the cartel model,
      a. each firm behaves like a price taker.
      b. the firms behave like a multiplant monopoly where each firm acts like a separate division of a single monopolistic firm.
      c. the firms follow a price leader.
      d. each firm observes a kinked demand curve.
      e. c and d.

38. _____ In the cartel model, the price will
      a. equal marginal cost, just as in the perfectly competitive case.
      b. exceed marginal cost, just as in the perfectly competitive case.
      c. equal marginal cost, just as in the monopoly case.
      d. exceed marginal cost, just as in the monopoly case.
      e. equal average cost always.

39. _____ Cartel agreements
      a. are often illegal.
      b. require little information to implement.
      c. are in the collective interests of cartel members.
      d. are inherently unstable because it is in the individual interest of each member to cheat on the agreement.
      e. a, c, and d.

40. _____ The price leadership model assumes that
      a. each firm acts independently.
      b. each firm acts like a single plant in a monopoly.
      c. all the firms follow the price set by a leader.
      d. all firms are price takers.
      e. a and d.

41. _____ The kinked demand model hypothesizes that each firm believes that other firms will
      a. follow when it increases its price.
      b. follow when it decreases its price.
      c. not follow when it increases its price.
      d. not follow when it decreases its price.
      e. b and c.

42. _____ In the Cournot model each firm assumes that
      a. the other firm's price will not change.
      b. the other firm's quantity will not change.
      c. the other firm's price and quantity will not change.
      d. the other firm's quantity may change.
      e. none of the above.

43. _____ A reaction function describes how one firm's
      a. price will change as the other firm's price changes.
      b. price will change as the other firm's quantity changes.
      c. quantity will change as the other firm's price changes.
      d. quantity will change as the other firm's quantity changes.
      e. profits will change as the other firm's profits change.

44. _____ At a Cournot equilibrium, the profits of the total industry are
      a. more than the monopoly case.
      b. less than the monopoly case.
      c. more than the competitive case.
      d. less than the competitive case.
      e. b and c.

45. _____ When oligopolies do not produce homogeneous goods,
      a. the industry will always act like a cartel.
      b. the industry will always act like a perfectly competitive industry.
      c. the decisions of one firm will not affect other firms in the industry.
      d. few general conclusions can be drawn.
      e. c and d.

46. _____ A firm engaging in constructive advertising is attempting to
      a. draw customers away from competitors.
      b. enlarge the market of the entire industry.
      c. drive competitors out of business.
      d. a and b.
      e. a, b, and c.

47. _____ In the long run, if there are no barriers to entry, economic profits
      a. must equal zero.
      b. must be positive.
      c. must be negative.
      d. may be positive, negative, or zero.
      e. must equal one.

48. _____ In contestable markets, the price must
      a. equal minimum average cost.
      b. equal marginal cost.
      c. equal average variable cost.
      d. exceed average cost.
      e. a and b.

RUNNING GLOSSARY

49. _____ Quasi-competitive model: a model of oligopoly pricing in which each firm acts as a price _____.

50. _____ _____ model: a model of oligopoly pricing in which firms coordinate their decisions to act as a multiplant monopoly.

51. _____
52. _____ Kinked demand curve model: a model in which firms believe that price _____ result in a very elastic demand while price decreases result in a(n) _____ demand for their products.

53. _____ Price _____ model: a model in which one dominant firm takes reactions of all other firms into account in its output and pricing decisions.

54. _____ Competitive fringe: a group of firms that act as price _____ in a market dominated by a price leader.

55. _____ Cournot model: a model of duopoly in which each firm assumes the other firm's _____ will not change if it changes its own output level.

56. _____ Reaction function: in the _____ model, a function or graph that shows how much one firm will produce given what the other firm produces.

57. _____ Cournot equilibrium: a solution to the Cournot model in which each firm makes the _____ assumption about what the other firm will produce.

58. _____ Product group: set of _____ products that are highly substitutable for one another.

59. _____ _____ products: the inseparable combination of two goods in production, with one being advertising for example, which is paid for by the consumer as part of the good being advertised.

60. _____ Monopolistic competition: market in which each firm faces a negatively sloped demand curve and there are _____ barriers to entry.

61. _____ Contestable market: market in which entry and exit are _____.

ANSWERS

1. two
2. takers
3. price
4. marginal
5. long
6. monopoly
7. less
8. exceed
9. collective
10. individual
11. oligopolistic
12. lowering
13. raise
14. costs
15. duopoly
16. output
17. given
18. Cournot
19. accurate
20. less
21. differentiate

22. are not
23. many
24. joint
25. less
26. combative
27. zero
28. equals
29. equal
30. price
31. less
32. marginal
33. minimum
34. d
35. a
36. a
37. b
38. d
39. e
40. c
41. e
42. b

43. d
44. e
45. d
46. b
47. a
48. e
49. taker
50. Cartel
51. increases
52. inelastic
53. leadership
54. takers
55. output
56. Cournot
57. correct
58. differentiated
59. Joint
60. no
61. costless

CHAPTER 12

STRATEGY AND GAME THEORY

LEARNING OBJECTIVES

- No player has an incentive to change his/her strategy when a Nash equilibrium exists.
- A dominant strategy is optimal regardless of what the other player does.
- A threat is credible only if the player has an incentive to follow through on the threat if the situation actually arises.
- A first mover can gain an advantage by incurring sunk costs thereby deterring the entry of others.

WALKING TOUR SUMMARY

BASIC CONCEPTS

1. _____
2. _____

3. _____

4. _____

Economists try to capture the strategic relationships by using _____ theory. In a game, each player chooses a course of action, a(n) _____. Each player's payoff not only depends on his/her strategy, but also on the strategies that _____ employ. The payoff matrix describes what a player's payoff will be depending on the strategies that he/she and others use. In a zero-sum game what one player wins, the other player _____. Most market situations are not zero sum, however.

EQUILIBRIUM CONCEPTS

5. _____

6. _____

The Nash equilibrium is the most frequently used equilibrium notion in game theory. At a Nash equilibrium, no player has an incentive to _____ his/her strategy assuming that the other players do not alter their strategies. Not all games have an equilibrium. Economists call such games nonequilibrium games. A particular strategy is _____ for a player, if that player is always better off by choosing the strategy regardless of what his opponent does.

THE PRISONER'S DILEMMA

In the prisoner's dilemma, there are two players. Each player's prison sentence depends on whether or not he/she confesses and also whether or not the other player confesses.

7. _____ The equilibrium occurs when both players _____. This outcome is second best, however, since each player could receive a lighter sentence if neither confessed.

8. _____ Unfortunately, this cooperative situation is _____. Each player has an incentive to cheat and confess if he/she believes that the other player will not confess. The behavior of a duopoly can be viewed as a prisoner's dilemma. The cooperative outcome in which industry profits are maximized is unstable because each firm has

9. _____ an incentive to _____.

Communication can help the players cooperate in order to avoid the second-best outcome. Also, if the game is played repeatedly, the prospect of cooperation is

10. _____ _____.

MANY PERIOD GAMES

Many period games reflect real-world markets

11. _____ _____ than single period games. A player can try to influence his opponent's strategy by issuing threats. A

12. _____ threat is _____ only if the player actually has an incentive to follow through on it should the situation arise. Consequently, players can eliminate strategies that involve noncredible threats in deciding their best course of action. A perfect equilibrium is a Nash equilibrium in which the

13. _____ strategy choices of each player do not involve _____

14. _____ threats. No strategy in a(n) _____ equilibrium requires a player to pursue an action that is not in his best interest at the time.

MODELS OF PRICING BEHAVIOR

At a Bertrand equilibrium, the firms share the market

15. _____ _____ for the homogeneous good. Each firm faces

16. _____ the _____ costs and charge a price equal to marginal cost. A Bertrand equilibrium is a Nash equilibrium. If the Bertrand assumptions regarding the homogeneity of the good and the firms' costs are not met, a

Bertrand equilibrium may not exist. In these situations, a

17. _____   _____ stage game may be played. The first stage
involves decision to entry and/or investment. The second

18. _____   stage involves _____ competition. The Cournot
equilibrium illustrates such a two-stage game in which firms

19. _____   first choose the quantity and then the _____. The
welfare implications of Bertrand and Cournot equilibria

20. _____   _____ dramatically. Since price equals marginal

21. _____   cost at a Bertrand equilibrium, _____ results. A
Cournot equilibrium produces monopoly-like inefficiencies

22. _____   because price _____ marginal cost.

When one adds the possibility of playing a Bertrand
game repeatedly, the welfare implications depend on the

23. _____   time horizon of the players. If the horizon is _____,
efficiency results; price will equal marginal cost, just as in
the single period case. On the other hand, price may

24. _____   _____ marginal cost in the infinite time horizon
case resulting in inefficiency.

ENTRY, EXIT, AND STRATEGY

When a firm contemplates entering a market, it must predict
how its entry will affect the price in subsequent periods.
To do so, it must consider how firms now in the industry

25. _____   will respond. A firm incurs _____ costs when
it invests in capital that cannot be shifted to other uses

26. _____   easily. Sunk costs provide _____ movers with an
advantage. By incurring sunk costs, a first mover stakes a
claim to a market by making a commitment. This

27. _____   commitment may deter potential rivals from _____
the industry. In particular, when production exhibits

28. _____   _____ returns to scale, the first mover may be able
to deter the entry of others by investing in a large-scale
operation.

The effectiveness of limit pricing as a method of entry

29. _____   deterrence must be questioned if _____ to entry are
not present. Incomplete information, however, could deter
entry. If potential entrants do not have as much information

30. _____   as the incumbent, entry could be deterred. _____
pricing refers to the deliberate use of low prices to drive
competitors out of business. While similar to limit pricing,

predatory pricing models stress the importance of asymmetric information.

N-PLAYER GAME THEORY

N-player games are more complicated than two-player games, because the number of potential coalitions is larger and the complexity of the payoff matrix expands rapidly
31. _____ as the number of players _____. The likelihood of
32. _____ successful coalitions depends upon _____ costs, costs associated with the information required to determine coalition strategies and the enforcement mechanism required to ensure that the chosen strategy is followed. When incentives to cheat are great, enforcement costs can be
33. _____ _____. If these costs are too high, successful coalitions will not be established.

MULTIPLE-CHOICE QUESTIONS

34. _____ A payoff matrix describes the
    a. salaries earned by a firm's workers.
    b. bribes collected by corrupt politicians.
    c. what a player's rewards will be in a game.
    d. the rewards of a college education.
    e. none of the above.

35. _____ A Nash equilibrium
    a. is a generalization of the Cournot equilibrium.
    b. exists in all games.
    c. exists in all zero-sum games.
    d. occurs when no player has an incentive to change when all strategies are unknown.
    e. none of the above.

36. _____ In a zero-sum game,
    a. what one player wins never equals what other players lose.
    b. what one player wins always equals what other players lose.
    c. at least one of the players never loses.
    d. each player must win nothing.
    e. none of the above.

37. _____ In a non-zero-sum game,
     a. one player wins twice as much as the other.
     b. what one player wins always equals what other players lose.
     c. at least one of the players never loses.
     d. each player must win nothing.
     e. none of the above.

38. _____ The prisoner's dilemma
     a. has no equilibrium.
     b. has a single equilibrium.
     c. illustrates the incentive players have to cheat.
     d. a and c.
     e. b and c.

39. _____ A Bertrand model assumes that firms
     a. are public spirited.
     b. face the same costs.
     c. act as a cartel.
     d. share the market equally if they charge the same price.
     e. b and d.

40. _____ At a Bertrand equilibrium,
     a. price equals marginal cost.
     b. price exceeds marginal cost.
     c. price is less than marginal cost.
     d. inefficiency results.
     e. b and d.

41. _____ At a Cournot equilibrium,
     a. price equals marginal cost.
     b. price exceeds marginal cost.
     c. price is less than marginal cost.
     d. inefficiency results.
     e. b and d.

42. _____ Sunk costs refer to
     a. all fixed costs.
     b. all variable costs.
     c. all investment in capital.
     d. all investment in capital that cannot be shifted to other uses easily.
     e. total costs.

RUNNING GLOSSARY

43. _____ Game: a simple representation of a strategic situation in which the outcome depends on what _____ player in the game does.

44. _____ _____: a participant in a game. May be an individual, a firm, or groups of individuals and firms.

45. _____ _____: the various courses of action open to the players of a game.

46. _____ Payoffs: the outcomes of a game for each player. Payoffs depend on what _____ have been chosen.

47. _____ _____ equilibrium: a choice of strategies by the players of a game such that once all the strategies are known, no player has an incentive to choose a different strategy.

48. _____ Zero-sum game: a game in which the amount one player loses the other player _____.

49. _____ _____ dilemma: a game in which the players' most desirable outcome is unstable because each player has an incentive to cheat in the strategy actually chosen.

50. _____ Credible threats: threats that the player has an incentive to _____ out if the situation arises.

51. _____ _____ equilibrium: a Nash equilibrium in which the strategy choices of the players do not involve noncredible threats.

52. _____ _____ costs: the costs incurred by a firm when it invests in capital that cannot be shifted to other uses easily.

53. _____ Predatory pricing: the deliberate use of _____ prices to drive competitors out of business.

ANSWERS

1. game
2. strategy
3. others
4. loses
5. change
6. dominant
7. confess
8. unstable
9. cheat
10. enhanced
11. better
12. credible
13. noncredible
14. perfect
15. equally
16. same
17. two
18. price

19. price
20. differ
21. efficiency
22. exceeds
23. finite
24. exceed
25. sunk
26. first
27. entering
28. increasing
29. barriers
30. Predatory
31. increases
32. organization
33. high
34. c
35. a
36. b

37. e
38. e
39. e
40. a
41. e
42. d
43. each
44. Player
45. Strategies
46. strategies
47. Nash
48. wins
49. Prisoner's
50. carry
51. Perfect
52. Sunk
53. low

PART 4

MODELS OF MARKET EQUILIBRIUM

WALKING TOUR PROBLEMS

FIRM AND INDUSTRY REACTIONS IN THE SHORT AND LONG RUN

1. Initially, a perfectly competitive market is in long-run equilibrium. Subsequently, the fixed costs of each firm increase.

   a. Initially, are profits of a typical firm in the industry positive, negative, or zero?

   1. _____

   2. _____

   3. _____

   4. _____

   Since the industry is in long-run equilibrium, the typical firm in the industry has _____ incentive to leave the industry; consequently, profits cannot be _____. Furthermore, no firm can have an incentive to _____ the industry; consequently, profits cannot be _____. Therefore, profits must be zero.

   The answer is zero.

   b. Initially, how is the price related to the typical firm's average cost?

   5. _____

   6. _____

   7. _____

   Profits for the typical firm are zero; hence, total revenue _____ total cost. Total revenue equals price times _____; total cost equals average cost times quantity. Price must _____ average cost.

   The answer is price equals average cost.

   c. In the short run, after fixed costs increase what happens to the market demand curve?

- 189 -

8. _____

The position of the market demand curve is _____ by the change in fixed costs.

The answer is nothing.

d. In the short run, after fixed costs increase what happens to each firm's marginal cost curve? Each firm's individual supply curve? The market supply curve?

9. _____

10. _____

Marginal cost equals the change in the firm's total cost as a consequence of producing _____ additional unit of output. The increase in fixed costs will _____ affect a firm's marginal cost curve.

The answer is nothing.

11. _____

12. _____

An individual firm's supply curve is its _____ cost curve (as long as price exceeds average variable costs). Since the change in fixed costs will not affect the firm's marginal cost curves, it will _____ affect their individual supply curves.

The answer is nothing.

13. _____

14. _____

The market supply curve is the _____ sum of each individual firm's supply curve. Since the individual supply curves are not affected, the market supply curve will _____ be affected.

The answer is nothing.

e. In the short run, after variable costs increase what happens to the price and quantity?

15. _____

16. _____

In a perfectly competitive market, the price and quantity are determined by the market _____ and supply curves. Neither the demand curve nor the supply curve has _____; consequently, the price and quantity are unchanged.

The answer is nothing.

f. What has happened to the typical firm's average cost curve? The typical firm's profits? Is the industry still in a long-run equilibrium? What happens in the long run?

Since fixed costs have risen, the average cost curve will shift _____.

17. _____

The answer is it has risen.

To determine the sign of profits, compare _____ and average cost. Initially, the price equals average cost. The increase in fixed costs leaves the price unchanged whereas average cost has risen; price is now less than average cost. Consequently, profits are now negative.

18. _____

The answer is profits are negative.

The industry is not in long-run equilibrium because the typical firm now earns _____ profits.

19. _____

The answer is no.

When profits are _____, the owners of firms can earn more from their resources by using them elsewhere in the economy. Consequently, firms will exit the industry in the long run.

20. _____

The answer is firms will exit.

g. In the long run, what happens to the market supply curve? The price and quantity?

The market supply curve is the horizontal sum of each firm's _____ supply curve. Since there are fewer firms in the industry, the market supply curve will shift to the _____.

21. _____

22. _____

The answer is it shifts to the left.

When the market supply curve shifts to the left, the equilibrium price _____ and the equilibrium quantity decreases.

23. _____

The answer is the price increases and the quantity decreases.

2. Initially, a perfectly competitive market is in long-run equilibrium. Subsequently, the variable costs of each firm increase raising the firm's marginal and average cost by $.10.

  a. Initially, are profits of a typical firm in the industry positive, negative, or zero?

24. _____ Since the industry is in _____-run equilibrium, the typical firm in the industry has no incentive to leave the industry; consequently, profits cannot be negative. Furthermore, no firm can have an incentive to enter the industry; consequently, _____
25. _____ cannot be positive. Therefore, _____ must be
26. _____ zero.

The answer is zero.

  b. Initially, how is the price related to the typical firm's average cost?

27. _____ Profits for the typical firm are _____; hence, total revenue equals total cost. Total revenue equals
28. _____ _____ times quantity; total cost equals
29. _____ _____ cost times quantity. Price must equal
30. _____ _____ cost.

The answer is price equals average cost.

  c. In the short run, after variable costs increase what happens to the market demand curve?

31. _____ The position of the market _____ curve is unaffected by the change in variable costs.

The answer is nothing.

  d. In the short run, after variable costs increase what happens to each firm's marginal cost curve? Each

Copyright © 2000 by Harcourt, Inc.   - 192 -

firm's individual supply curve? The market supply curve?

The increase in variable costs shifts each firm's marginal cost curve up by $.10.

The answer is shift up by $.10.

32. _____

33. _____

An individual firm's _____ curve is its marginal cost curve (as long as price exceeds average _____ costs). The change in variable costs will shift each firm's individual supply curve up by $.10.

The answer is shift up by $.10.

34. _____

35. _____

The market supply curve is the horizontal sum of each _____ firm's supply curve; consequently, the market supply curve will shift _____ by $.10.

The answer is shift up by $.10.

e. In the short run, after fixed costs increase what happens to the price and quantity?

36. _____

37. _____

38. _____

In a perfectly competitive market, the equilibrium price and quantity are determined by the _____ demand and supply curves. Since the demand curve has remained stationary and the supply curve has shifted up, the quantity will _____ and the price will increase. The price will rise by less than $_____, however, because the supply curve has shifted up by only $.10.

The answer is the price increases by less than $.10 and the quantity decreases.

f. What has happened to the typical firm's average cost curve? The typical firm's profits?   Is the industry still in a long-run equilibrium? What happens in the long run?

The average cost curve has shifted up by $.10.

The answer is it has risen by $.10.

To determine the sign of profits, compare price and average cost. The price has risen by _____ than $.10. Since price equaled average costs initially, price is now _____ than average cost. Consequently, profits are now negative.

39. _____

40. _____

The answer is negative.

The industry is not in long-run equilibrium because the typical firm now earns _____ profits.

41. _____

The answer is no.

42. _____

When profits are _____, the owners of firms can earn more from their resources by using them elsewhere in the economy. Consequently, firms will exit the industry in the long run.

The answer is firms will exit.

g. In the long run, what happens to the market supply curve? The price and quantity?

43. _____

44. _____

The market supply curve is the horizontal sum of each firm's _____ supply curve. Since there are fewer firms in the industry, the market supply curve will shift to the _____.

The answer is it shifts to the left.

45. _____

When the market supply curve shifts to the left, the equilibrium price _____ and the equilibrium quantity decreases.

The answer is the price increases and the quantity decreases.

3. Initially, a perfectly competitive market is in long-run equilibrium. Subsequently, there is an increase in demand.

a. Initially, are profits of a typical firm in the industry positive, negative, or zero?

46. _____

b. Initially, how is the price related to the typical firm's average cost?

47. _____

c. In the short run, what happens to the market demand curve?

48. _____

d. In the short run, what happens to each firm's marginal cost curve? What happens to each firm's individual supply curve? What happens to the market supply curve?

49. _____
50. _____
51. _____

e. In the short run, what happens to the price? What happens to the quantity?

52. _____
53. _____

f. What has happened to the typical firm's average cost curve? What happens to the profits earned by the typical firm? What happens to the profits in the long run?

54. _____
55. _____
56. _____

g. In the long run, what happens to the market supply curve? In the long run, what happens to the price? In the long run, what happens to the quantity?

57. _____
58. _____
59. _____

ANSWERS

1. no	21. individual	41. negative
2. negative	22. left	42. negative
3. enter	23. increases	43. individual
4. positive	24. long	44. left
5. equals	25. profits	45. increases
6. quantity	26. profits	46. zero
7. equal	27. zero	47. equal
8. unaffected	28. price	48. shifts right
9. one	29. average	49. nothing
10. not	30. average	50. nothing
11. marginal	31. demand	51. nothing
12. not	32. supply	52. increases
13. horizontal	33. variable	53. decreases
14. not	34. individual	54. nothing
15. demand	35. up	55. become positive
16. shifted	36. market	56. firms enter
17. up	37. decrease	57. shifts right
18. price	38. .10	58. decreases
19. negative	39. less	59. decreases
20. negative	40. less	

PART 5

FURTHER TOPICS

CHAPTER 13

GENERAL EQUILIBRIUM

LEARNING OBJECTIVES
- The perfectly competitive model assumes that there are a large number of
    1. utility-maximizing individuals buying goods and supplying goods;
    2. profit-maximizing firms producing each good and purchasing each input.

  Also, all individuals and firms take prices as given.
- Efficiency in production: The production possibility frontier illustrates all technically efficient combinations of goods.
- The rate of product transformation reflects how one good can be "transformed" into another good; geometrically, it is illustrated by the slope of the production possibility frontier.
- An individual's marginal rate of substitution reflects how the individual can substitute one good for another while remaining just as well off.
- An efficient mix of goods is being produced whenever the marginal rate of substitution equals the rate of product transformation.
- Perfect competition results in efficiency in the absence of externalities and public goods.

WALKING TOUR SUMMARIES

PERFECTLY COMPETITIVE PRICE SYSTEM

The perfectly competitive model assumes that:

1. _____

2. _____

1. There is a(n) _____ number of people buying each good and supplying each productive input. Each individual takes all _____ as given and maximizes his utility.

3. _____
4. _____

5. _____

2. There is a(n) _____ number of firms producing each _____ and purchasing each productive input. Each firm takes all prices as given and maximizes its _____.

6. _____

7. _____
8. _____

Instead of considering a single market in isolation, general equilibrium studies the interconnection of the markets for goods and inputs. Typically, a change in demand and/or supply in one market will ultimately affect _____ other markets. For example, if the demand for one particular good increases, the price of that good _____. The incomes of workers producing the good will _____, and consequently their demand for all other goods will be affected. This of course will affect the prices of other goods and the incomes of workers producing those goods.

EFFICIENCY IN PRODUCTION

9. _____

10. _____

When resources are allocated efficiently, the only way to increase the production of one good is to _____ the production of some other good. Resources are allocated inefficiently if more of one good can be produced _____ producing less of any other good.

PRODUCTION POSSIBILITY FRONTIER

11. _____

The production possibility frontier illustrates the alternative outputs of X and Y that can be produced with the fixed amounts of inputs available to an economy. An economy operating at a point inside its production possibility frontier is operating _____ because the production of one

12. _____

13. _____

good can be increased without reducing the production of the other good. An economy operating _____ the frontier is efficient; the only way to produce more of one good is to _____ the production of the other good.

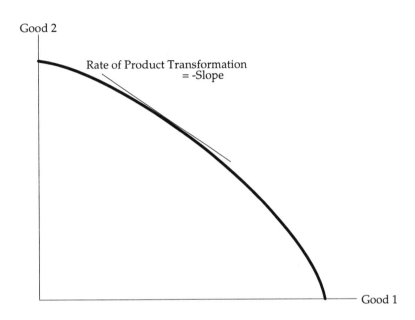

Figure 13.1: *Production Possibility Curve*

RATE OF PRODUCT TRANSFORMATION IS THE RATIO OF MARGINAL COSTS

The rate of product transformation (RPT) indicates how the production of good X can be substituted for the production of good Y given the fixed amount of resources available to an economy. Geometrically, the _____ of the production possibility frontier reflects the rate of product transformation. The rate of product transformation equals the _____ of marginal costs:

14. _____

15. _____

$$RPT = \frac{\text{Marginal Cost of Good X}}{\text{Marginal Cost of Good Y}}$$

To understand why suppose that the MC_X equals 6 and the MC_Y equals 2. To produce one additional unit of good X, _____ dollars worth of inputs must be transferred from the production of Y to the production of X. The production of Y decreases by one unit when _____

16. _____

17. _____

18. _____ dollars worth of inputs are taken because the MC_Y equals 2. Thus, the production of Y will fall by _____ units when six dollars worth of inputs are taken. Consequently, the rate of product transformation equals (6/2) or 3.

The rate of product transformation increases as more X is produced. When little X and much Y are produced, the MC_X is low and the MC_Y is high; thus, the ratio of MCs is

19. _____ _____. Alternatively, when much X and little Y are produced, the MC_X is high and the MC_Y is low; the ratio is

20. _____ _____. The rate of product transformation equals the

21. _____ _____ cost of X; that is, how much Y that must be forgone to produce one additional unit of X.

AN EFFICIENT MIX OF OUTPUTS

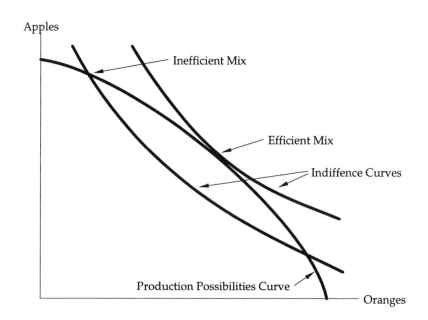

Figure 13.2: *Efficient Output Mix*

The production of an efficient mix of output requires the rate of product transformation (RPT) to equal the

22. _____ individuals' marginal rates of _____ (MRS). To understand why, assume that they are not equal; for example, suppose that the RPT of oranges for apples equals 1 and that an individual's MRS equals 3. Recall that an individual's marginal rate of substitution indicates the ratio

23. _____ in which the individual is willing to _____ oranges for apples. Since the MRS equals 3, the individual is willing

24. _____ to give up _____ apples to consume one additional

25. _____

orange. But if the rate of product transformation equals 1, it is only necessary to reduce apple production by _____ to grow the additional orange. More oranges and fewer apples should be grown in this case. Whenever the RPT and MRS's are not equal, the mix of output is

26. _____ _____ .

EFFICIENCY OF PERFECT COMPETITION

27. _____

In order to maximize utility, each individual will consume a bundle of goods at which the individual's marginal rate of _____ equals the price ratio; that is,

$$MRS = \frac{P_X}{P_Y}$$

28. _____
29. _____

In order to maximize profits, a firm produces the level of output at which marginal revenue equals marginal _____. In a perfectly competitive industry, _____ equals marginal revenue; therefore, price will equal marginal cost for a profit-maximizing firm in a

30. _____ _____ competitive industry:

$$P_X = MR_X = MC_X$$
$$P_Y = MR_Y = MC_Y$$

31. _____

Thus, the marginal rate of substitution that equals the price ratio also equals the ratio of marginal _____; that is,

$$MRS = \frac{P_X}{P_Y} = \frac{MR_X}{MR_Y} = \frac{MC_X}{MC_Y}$$

Now recall that the ratio of marginal costs equals the rate of product transformation:

$$MRS = \frac{P_X}{P_Y} = \frac{MR_X}{MR_Y} = \frac{MC_X}{MC_Y} = RPT$$

32. _____

The marginal rate of substitution equals the rate of product transformation ensuring that a(n) _____ output mix will be produced.

PRICES, EFFICIENCY, AND LAISSEZ-FAIRE POLICIES

33. _____

A perfectly competitive price system composed of profit-maximizing firms and utility-maximizing consumers can result in a(n) _____ allocation of resources. Note that in justifying this conclusion we relied on the assumption that each party will pursue his self-interest; each firm maximizes its profit and each individual maximizes his/her utility. What then is the role for government?

WHY MARKETS FAIL TO ACHIEVE ECONOMIC EFFICIENCY

34. _____

_____ competition typically leads to inefficiency. Like any firm, a firm in an imperfectly competitive industry maximizes profit by producing the level of output

35. _____

at which marginal revenue equals _____ cost. Price exceeds a firm's marginal revenue in an imperfectly competitive market, however. Consequently, price will

36. _____

_____ marginal cost; for example, if the market for good X is imperfectly competitive:

$$P_X > MR_X = MC_X$$

37. _____

This of course means that the consumer's marginal rates of substitution (which equal the _____ ratio) will no longer equal the rate of product transformation (which

38. _____

equals the ratio of marginal _____); an inefficient output mix results.

$$MRS = \frac{P_X}{P_Y} > \frac{MR_X}{MR_Y} = \frac{MC_X}{MC_Y} = RPT$$

39. _____

Inefficiency also results in the case of an externality; that is, when the price system fails to capture _____ the relationships among firms and/or consumers. For example, whenever a firm emits air pollution those individuals living nearby are hurt by the dirty air, yet the firm incurs no charge for this damage. The price system fails to capture the fact that the firm by emitting pollutants is hurting those living nearby. Consequently, the

40. _____

_____ costs, the costs upon which the firm bases its output decisions, are less than the true social costs of production; the ratio of private marginal costs will no longer

41. _____ equal the rate of _____ transformation. An inefficient output mix results because the individual's marginal rates of substitution (which equal the price ratio

42. _____ and ratio of marginal _____ costs) do not equal the rate of product transformation.

Public goods also cause market failure. Because it is impossible (or at least very costly) to exclude anyone from enjoying the benefits of public goods, there is an incentive for each individual to refuse to pay for them. Too few public goods are provided by the price system.

EFFICIENCY AND EQUITY

43. _____ People _____ on what they regard as "fair." Some Americans find the current distribution of income equitable, while others find it grossly unfair. But even if everyone agreed on what was fair, there might still be a problem in obtaining a fair outcome. There may not be a

44. _____ _____ to get the economy from the initial endowments to a fair outcome. For example, a system of

45. _____ _____ trades upon which perfect competition relies need not lead to a fair result. The government could use its power to transfer income to achieve equity. Such transfer

46. _____ programs typically result in _____ losses, however.

MONEY IN A PERFECTLY COMPETITIVE MODEL

Money facilitates transactions by providing a medium of

47. _____ _____ and acts as a store of value. Since all prices are quoted in terms of money, money serves as an accounting standard. The choice of the accounting standard

48. _____ does not affect _____ prices, but does affect

49. _____ _____ prices. If a commodity is chosen as the

50. _____ monetary standard, the _____ price of money is determined like any other relative price, by the forces of demand and supply. In the case of fiat money, the

51. _____ _____ is the sole supplier.

MULTIPLE-CHOICE QUESTIONS

52._____ The perfectly competitive model assumes that there is a
   a. large number of people purchasing each good.
   b. small number of people purchasing each good.
   c. large number of people supplying each productive input.
   d. small number of people supplying each productive input.
   e. a and c.

53._____ The perfectly competitive model assumes that there is a
   a. large number of firms producing each good.
   b. small number of firms producing each good.
   c. large number of firms purchasing productive inputs.
   d. small number of firms purchasing productive inputs.
   e. a and c.

54._____ The perfectly competitive model assumes that each
   a. person takes most, but not necessarily all, prices as given.
   b. firm takes no prices as given.
   c. firm takes most, but not necessarily all, prices as given.
   d. firm takes all prices as given.
   e. a and d.

55._____ The perfectly competitive model assumes that each
   a. individual maximizes utility.
   b. individual maximizes profit.
   c. firm maximizes utility.
   d. firm maximizes profit.
   e. a and d.

56._____ A change in demand in one market will typically affect
   a. only that market.
   b. that market and at most one or two other markets.
   c. that market and other markets only if the good involved is inferior.
   d. that market and many other markets.
   e. only markets of normal goods.

57._____ General equilibrium studies
   a. each market in isolation.
   b. several markets in isolation.
   c. how a small number of markets interact with each other.
   d. how all markets interact with each other.
   e. a and c.

58._____ When the economy is technically efficient
  a. additional production of one good can be achieved without reducing the production of other goods.
  b. it is impossible to increase the production of any good.
  c. additional production of one good can be achieved only by reducing the production of some other good.
  d. the production of all goods can be increased simultaneously.
  e. a and d.

59._____ The production possibility frontier illustrates the
  a. combinations of labor and capital that a firm can use to produce a given amount of output.
  b. alternative outputs of two goods that can be produced with the fixed amounts of inputs available to an economy.
  c. combinations of two goods that would provide a consumer with a given amount of utility.
  d. combinations of labor and capital that would provide a consumer with a given level of utility.
  e. b and c.

60._____ If an economy is operating at a point on its production possibility frontier
  a. production efficiency is guaranteed.
  b. an efficient mix of outputs is guaranteed.
  c. each individual's marginal rate of substitution is equal.
  d. each firm is operating at minimum marginal cost.
  e. a and d.

61._____ The rate of product transformation indicates how
  a. a firm can substitute labor for capital while keeping production constant.
  b. production of one good can be substituted for the production of another.
  c. an individual is willing to substitute the consumption of one good for another.
  d. a firm can substitute the production of one good today for the production of that good in the future.
  e. a and d.

62._____ The rate of product transformation is indicated by the slope of
  a. a firm's isoquant.
  b. a firm's indifference curve.
  c. the production possibility curve.
  d. a consumer's isoquant curve.
  e. a consumer's indifference curve.

63._____ The rate of product transformation equals the ratio of
  a. marginal utilities.
  b. the rates of technical substitution.
  c. marginal revenue.
  d. marginal cost.
  e. b and d.

64._____ The production of an efficient mix of outputs requires
  a. each consumer to have the same rate of technical substitution.
  b. each firm to have the same marginal rate of substitution.
  c. equality of the rates of technical substitution and the marginal rates of substitution.
  d. equality of the rates of technical substitution and the rate of product transformation.
  e. equality of the marginal rates of substitution and the rate of product transformation.

65._____ When a firm takes prices as given and maximizes profits
  a. the price of its output will equal its marginal revenue.
  b. its marginal revenue will equal its marginal cost.
  c. the price of its output will equal its marginal cost.
  d. it produces at minimum marginal cost.
  e. a, b, and c.

66._____ When each firm takes prices as given and maximizes profits,
  a. the price ratio must equal the ratio of marginal costs.
  b. the price ratio equals the rate of product transformation.
  c. an efficient mix of outputs is guaranteed.
  d. a and b.
  e. a, b, and c.

67._____   The marginal rate of substitution indicates
   a. how a firm can substitute labor for capital while keeping production constant.
   b. how production of one good can be substituted for the production of another.
   c. how an individual is willing to substitute the consumption of one good for another.
   d. how a firm can substitute the production of a good today with the production of that good in the future.
   e. a and c.

68._____   The marginal rate of substitution is indicated by the slope of
   a. a firm's isoquant.
   b. a firm's indifference curve.
   c. the production possibility curve.
   d. a consumer's isoquant curve.
   e. a consumer's indifference curve.

69._____   When each consumer takes prices as given and maximizes utility,
   a. the price ratio must equal the ratio of marginal costs.
   b. the price ratio must equal the rates of technical substitution.
   c. the price ratio must equal the marginal rates of substitution.
   d. an efficient mix of output is guaranteed.
   e. c and d.

70._____   When each firm takes prices as given and maximizes profit and also each consumer takes prices as given and maximizes utility,
   a. an efficient mix of output is guaranteed.
   b. efficient exchange is guaranteed.
   c. efficiency in production is guaranteed.
   d. a and b.
   e. a, b, and c.

71._____   Which typically leads to inefficiency in markets?
   a. imperfect competition
   b. externalities
   c. public goods
   d. a, b, and c
   e. none of the above

RUNNING GLOSSARY

72. _____

73. _____

Perfectly competitive price system: an economic model in which individuals maximize _____, firms maximize profits, information concerning prices is freely available, and every economic actor is a price _____.

74. _____ _____ efficient allocation of resources: an allocation of available resources such that producing more of one good requires producing less of some other good.

75. _____

76. _____

Production possibility frontier: a figure illustrating the technically efficient _____ possibilities for an economy with fixed amounts of _____.

77. _____

78. _____

Rate of product transformation: the slope of the _____ possibility frontier that shows the _____ costs involved in producing more of one good and less of some other good.

79. _____

Imperfect competition: a market situation in which buyers or sellers have some influence on the _____ of goods or services.

80. _____ _____: the effect of one party's economic activities on another party's well-being that is not taken into account by the price system.

81. _____

Public goods: goods that provide nonexclusive benefits to everyone in a group and that can be provided to one more user at _____ marginal cost.

82. _____

Equity: the _____ of the distribution of goods or utility.

83. _____

Initial endowments: the _____ holdings of goods from which trading begins.

ANSWERS

1. large
2. prices
3. large
4. good
5. profit
6. all
7. increases
8. increase
9. reduce
10. without
11. inefficiently
12. on
13. reduce
14. slope
15. ratio
16. 6
17. 2
18. 3
19. low
20. high
21. opportunity
22. substitution
23. trade
24. three
25. one
26. inefficient
27. substitution
28. cost

29. price
30. perfectly
31. costs
32. efficient
33. efficient
34. Imperfect
35. marginal
36. exceed
37. price
38. costs
39. all
40. private
41. product
42. private
43. disagree
44. mechanism
45. voluntary
46. efficiency
47. exchange
48. relative
49. absolute
50. relative
51. government
52. e
53. e
54. d
55. e
56. d

57. d
58. c
59. b
60. a
61. b
62. c
63. d
64. e
65. e
66. d
67. c
68. e
69. c
70. e
71. d
72. utility
73. taker
74. Technically
75. output
76. input
77. production
78. opportunity
79. prices
80. Externality
81. zero
82. fairness
83. initial

APPENDIX TO CHAPTER 13

THE EDGEWORTH BOX DIAGRAM

LEARNING OBJECTIVES

- The Edgeworth box for production illustrates all the ways to allocate two inputs between two firms.
- All points lying on the production possibility frontier are technically efficient.
- The Edgeworth box for consumption illustrates all the ways to allocate two goods between two consumers.

WALKING TOUR SUMMARIES

TECHNICAL EFFICIENCY AND THE RATE OF TECHNICAL SUBSTITUTION

1. _____

2. _____

A firm's rate of technical substitution (RTS) indicates how the firm can substitute labor for capital while keeping production _____. Technical efficiency requires the rate of technical substitution to be _____ for each good produced.

To understand why suppose that the rates are not equal; for example, suppose that the RTS for cars is 2 while the RTS for trucks is 1. Now shift one unit of labor from the production of trucks to cars and simultaneously shift one unit of capital from cars to trucks.

| Cars | ← | 1 labor | ← | Trucks |
| RTS = 2 | → | 1 capital | → | RTS = 1 |

Car production remains constant whenever 1 labor is substituted for 2 capital

Truck production remains constant whenever 1 labor is substituted for 1 capital

3. _____

4. _____

For trucks there is one less unit of labor and one more unit of capital; truck production will not be _____. Since the RTS is 1 for trucks, production remains constant whenever _____ unit of labor is substituted for one

unit of capital. For cars there is one more unit of labor and
5. _____ one less unit of capital; car production will _____.
Since the RTS is 2 for cars, production remains constant
6. _____ whenever _____ units of capital are substituted for
one unit of labor; hence, production will increase whenever
only one unit of capital is exchanged for one unit of labor.

THE EDGEWORTH BOX FOR PRODUCTION

The Edgeworth Box provides a graphical means to illustrate
7. _____ all the possible ways to _____ two inputs between
two firms. A particular point in the box represents
8. _____ _____ input use only when the isoquants passing
through the point are tangent. When the isoquants are
9. _____ tangent, the rates of _____ substitution are equal. If
the isoquants intersect, the rates of technical substitution are
10. _____ not equal. The firms can produce more of _____
goods by reallocating the inputs between them.

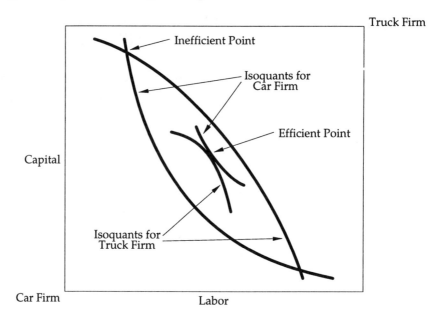

Figure 13a.1: *Edgeworth Production Box*

PRODUCTION POSSIBILITY CURVE

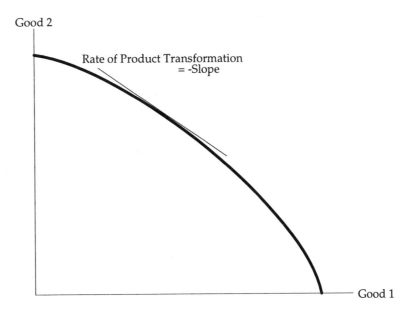

Figure 13a.2: *Production Possibility Curve*

The production possibility frontier illustrates the alternative outputs of X and Y that can be produced with the fixed amounts of inputs available to an economy. An economy operating at a point inside its production

11. _____ possibility frontier is operating _____ because the production of one good can be increased without reducing the production of the other good. An economy operating

12. _____ _____ the frontier is efficient; the only way to

13. _____ produce more of one good is to _____ the production of the other good.

MUTUALLY BENEFICIAL TRADES

An individual's marginal rate of substitution (MRS) equals the ratio at which he is willing to substitute two goods. Whenever two individuals have different marginal rates of substitution both can gain from trade. If they exchange the goods in a ratio between their marginal rates

14. _____ of _____, both will become better off. To understand why, assume that Smith's MRS of apples for oranges is 5 and Jones' is 1. Now, tell Smith to give Jones three oranges in exchange for one apple:

```
        Smith  ──────────▶  3 oranges  ──────────▶  Jones
    MRS = 5  ◀──────────     1 apple    ◀──────────  MRS = 1
      Smith is willing to                  Jones is willing to
      substitute 5 oranges                 substitute 1 orange
         for 1 apple                          for 1 apple
```

15. _____ Since Smith's MRS equals 5, exchanging _____ oranges for one apple would leave Smith just as well off. Smith only gives up three oranges, however; Smith becomes better off. Jones becomes better off, also. Since Jones' MRS

16. _____ equals 1, exchanging _____ apple for one orange would leave Jones just as well off. Jones actually receives

17. _____ three apples for one orange, however; Jones becomes _____ off, too.

While both individuals can benefit from voluntary trade, they need not share the gains equally. They typically negotiate the precise ratio at which the trade occurs. Each argues for those terms that most benefit him. Their skills as

18. _____ negotiators determine the _____ of the gains.

EDGEWORTH BOX DIAGRAM FOR EXCHANGE

The Edgeworth Box provides a graphical means to illustrate

19. _____ all the possible ways to _____ two goods between two individuals. The height of an Edgeworth Box represents the total amount of good Y owned by both individuals. The width represents the total amount of good X owned. The locus of all efficient points in the Edgeworth

20. _____ Box is called the _____ curve. If a point is not on the contract curve, the marginal rates of substitution are not equal. It is possible for the individuals to exchange the

21. _____ goods to make both of them _____ off. If a point is on the contract curve, however, the marginal rates of

22. _____ substitution are _____. The only way to make one person better off is to hurt the other.

MULTIPLE-CHOICE QUESTIONS

23._____ The rate of technical substitution indicates how
   a. a firm can substitute labor for capital while keeping production constant.
   b. production of one good can be substituted for the production of another.
   c. an individual is willing to substitute the consumption of one good for another.
   d. an individual is willing to substitute the consumption of goods today for the consumption of goods in the future.
   e. c and d.

24._____ The rate of technical substitution is indicated by the slope of
   a. a firm's isoquant.
   b. a firm's indifference curve.
   c. the production possibility curve.
   d. a consumer's isoquant curve.
   e. a consumer's indifference curve.

25._____ Technical efficiency requires
   a. each firm to have the same rate of technical substitution.
   b. each firm to have the same marginal rate of substitution.
   c. each consumer to have the same marginal rate of substitution.
   d. equality of the rates of technical substitution and the marginal rates of substitution.
   e. a and c.

26. _____ The marginal rate of substitution indicates
   a. how a firm can substitute labor for capital while keeping production constant.
   b. how production of one good can be substituted for the production of another.
   c. how an individual is willing to substitute the consumption of one good for another.
   d. how a firm can substitute the production of a good today with the production of that good in the future.
   e. a and c.

27. _____ The marginal rate of substitution is indicated by the slope of
    a. a consumer's compensated demand curve.
    b. a firm's indifference curve.
    c. the production possibility curve.
    d. a consumer's ordinary demand curve.
    e. a consumer's indifference curve.

28. _____ Whenever two individuals have different marginal rates of substitution, trade between them
    a. can help both.
    b. must help both.
    c. must hurt both.
    d. must hurt at least one.
    e. only helps one.

29. _____ Assume that Mr. Smith's marginal rate of substitution of good X for good Y is 2 and that Mr. Jones' is 5. If Mr. Smith trades one unit of good X to Mr. Jones in exchange for three units of good Y,
    a. both Mr. Smith and Mr. Jones will be helped.
    b. both Mr. Smith and Mr. Jones will be hurt.
    c. Mr. Smith will be helped, Mr. Jones hurt.
    d. Mr. Smith will be hurt, Mr. Jones helped.
    e. it is impossible to tell if either is helped or hurt.

30. _____ Assume that Mr. Smith's marginal rate of substitution of good X for good Y is 2 and that Mr. Jones' is 5. If Mr. Smith trades one unit of good X to Mr. Jones in exchange for one unit of good Y,
    a. both Mr. Smith and Mr. Jones will be helped.
    b. both Mr. Smith and Mr. Jones will be hurt.
    c. Mr. Smith will be helped, Mr. Jones hurt.
    d. Mr. Smith will be hurt, Mr. Jones helped.
    e. it is impossible to tell if either is helped or hurt.

31. _____ An Edgeworth box illustrates
    a. all the possible ways to divide income between two individuals.
    b. all the possible ways to divide utility between two individuals.
    c. all the possible ways to divide two goods between two individuals.
    d. all the inefficient ways to divide two goods between two individuals.
    e. none of the above.

32. _____ The contract curve illustrates
   a. the efficient ways to divide two goods between two individuals.
   b. the efficient ways to divide income between two individuals.
   c. each individual's demand curve.
   d. all points where the individual's marginal rates of substitution are equal.
   e. a and d.

RUNNING GLOSSARY

33. _____ _____ box diagram: a graphic device for illustrating all the possible allocations of two goods (or two inputs) that are in fixed supply.

34. _____ Pareto _____ allocation: an allocation of available resources in which no mutually beneficial trading opportunities are unexploited. That is, an allocation in which no one person can be made better off without
35. _____ someone else being made _____ off.

36. _____ Contract curve: the set of all _____ allocations of the existing goods in an exchange situation. Points off that curve are necessarily inefficient, since individuals can be made unambiguously better off by moving to the curve.

ANSWERS

1. constant	13. reduce	25. a
2. equal	14. substitution	26. c
3. affected	15. five	27. e
4. one	16. one	28. a
5. increase	17. better	29. a
6. two	18. distribution	30. d
7. allocate	19. allocate	31. c
8. efficient	20. contract	32. e
9. technical	21. better	33. Edgeworth
10. both	22. equal	34. efficient
11. inefficiently	23. a	35. worse
12. on	24. a	36. efficient

CHAPTER 14

PRICING IN INPUT MARKETS

LEARNING OBJECTIVES

- The marginal revenue product of an input equals the change in the firm's total revenue resulting from a one unit change in the input.
- The marginal expense of an input equals the change in the firm's total costs resulting from a one unit change in the input.
- Profit maximizing firms will hire an input until the marginal revenue product of the input equals its marginal expense.
- When the price of one input rises, firms respond in two ways: firms substitute other inputs for the one that became more expensive and firms produce less output because production has become more costly.
- Monopsony occurs whenever only one firm demands a particular input.
- Compared to perfect competition, monopsony results in a lower input price.

WALKING TOUR SUMMARIES

MARGINAL PRODUCTIVITY THEORY OF FACTOR DEMAND

1. _____

2. _____

3. _____

A profit-maximizing firm will hire an input until the marginal revenue product _____ the marginal expense. The marginal revenue product of labor (MR_L) equals the change in total revenue resulting from the use of one additional unit of _____. The marginal expense of labor (ME_L) equals the change in total _____ resulting from the employment of one additional unit of labor.

MARGINAL REVENUE PRODUCT OF LABOR

4. _____   The marginal revenue product of labor equals marginal physical product (MR$_L$) _____ marginal revenue (MR):

$$MR_L = MP_L \times MR$$

5. _____   Marginal physical product of labor equals the change in total _____ resulting from the use of one additional unit of labor. Marginal revenue equals the change in total revenue resulting from the sale of one additional unit of

6. _____   _____. When a firm hires one additional unit of

7. _____   labor, total _____ increases by MP$_L$ units. When sold, each additional unit of output increases total

8. _____   _____ by MR dollars. Consequently, MP$_L$ additional

9. _____   units of output will increase total _____ by MP$_L \times$ MR.

MARGINAL EXPENSE OF LABOR

10. _____   If a firm is a price taker in the labor market, the marginal expense of labor _____ the wage rate:

$$ME_L = w$$

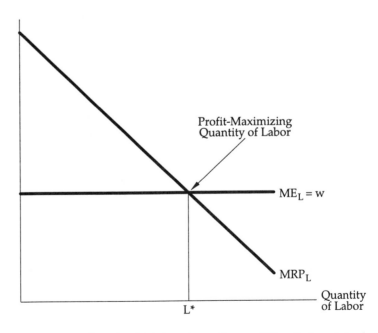

Figure 14.1: *Profit Maximizing in a Competitive Labor Market*

To summarize, a profit-maximizing firm that is a price taker in the labor market will hire labor until

$$w = ME_L = MR_L = MP_L \times MR$$

A SPECIAL CASE: MARGINAL VALUE PRODUCT

11. _____

12. _____

The marginal value product of labor (MVP_L) equals the value of the additional output that a firm produces when it hires one additional unit of _____. Marginal value product equals marginal physical product times the _____ of output:

$$MVP_L = MP_L \times P$$

13. _____

14. _____

If the firm is selling its output in a competitive market, then marginal revenue product _____ marginal value product because marginal revenue equals _____:

$$MVP_L = MP_L \times P = MP_L \times MR = MR_L$$

RESPONSES TO CHANGES IN INPUT PRICES

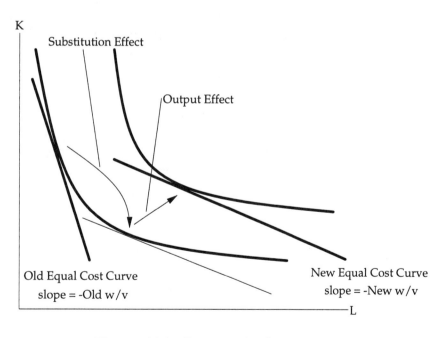

Figure 14.2: *Decrease in the Wage Rate*

15. _____

16. _____

In the single input case, a fall in the wage rate reduces the marginal _____ of labor because the marginal expense of labor equals the wage rate. The firm reacts by hiring _____ labor.

17. _____

18. _____

19. _____

20. _____

21. _____

In the two input case, a fall in the wage rate leads to two effects, a substitution effect and an output effect. The _____ in the wage rate reduces the ratio of the wage rate to the rental rate of capital. Thus, at a constant level of output the cost minimizing combination of labor and capital changes. As a result of the _____ effect, the firm substitutes the now cheaper labor for capital and thereby uses more labor and less capital. Of course, we would not expect the firm's level of output to remain constant when the wage rate falls. A change in the wage rate typically shifts the firm's cost curves. A downward shift in the firm's _____ cost curve would increase the profit-maximizing level of production. To produce more the firm would move along its expansion path. Assuming that labor is not a(n) _____ input, the firm would use more labor as a result of the _____ effect.

22. _____

23. _____

24. _____

The size of the substitution effect depends on how easy it is for firms to _____ for labor. If it is easy to substitute for labor, the substitution effect will be _____. If it is difficult, the substitution effect will be small. The size of the output effect depends on how much the _____ cost curves of firms will shift when the wage changes.

INPUT SUPPLY

25. _____

26. _____

Broadly speaking, firms use three types of inputs: labor, capital, and natural resources. The _____ curves for capital and natural resources are similar to the supply curve for products firms produce; that is, the supply curves are typically upward sloping. The supply curve for _____ is more complicated, however, because it involves decisions of individuals rather than firms. While these decisions can be complicated to analyze, the supply curve for labor is usually upward sloping.

MONOPSONY

There are situations in which a firm is not a price taker for the inputs that it hires. A monopsony (a single buyer) is the polar case of such a situation. Because the monopsonist is the sole purchaser, he/she is aware of the

27. _____ _____ curve. The monopsonist realizes that when he/she hires more of the input, he/she must offer a

28. _____ _____ price. Otherwise, the quantity supplied will not change.

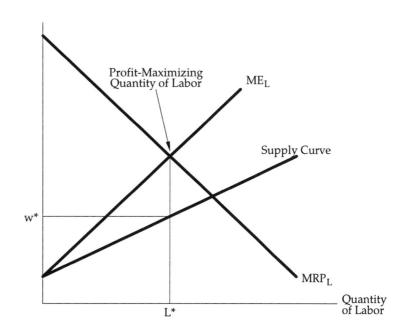

Figure 14.3: *Profit Maximizing Monopsonist*

In this case the marginal expense of the input will

29. _____ _____ the input's price. To explain why recall the definition of the marginal expense of labor. The marginal expense of labor equals the change in firm's total costs when it hires one additional unit of labor. Unlike a price taker, the

30. _____ monopsonist must offer a(n) _____ wage to hire the additional unit of labor. This has two effects on total costs. As a result of the additional unit of labor itself, total costs

31. _____ rise by an amount equal to the _____. The firm, however, must also pay the higher wage to all other workers. Labor costs for the other workers will

32. _____ _____. Total costs will rise by an amount greater

33. _____ than the _____. When the monopsonist maximizes profits, its marginal revenue product of labor will

34. _____ _____ the wage:

$$w < ME_L = MR_L$$

The most frequently cited examples of monopsonies are company towns, towns in which there is only a single employer. In an geographically isolated town with a single employer, workers have little choice. They have only

35. _____ _____ potential source of employment. Similarly, specialized employment skills can also limit a worker's sources of possible employment. If a profit-maximizing firm has a monopsony in two input markets, it often has an

36. _____ incentive to _____ between the groups. Typically, it

37. _____ will pay the groups different _____ even though the groups may be equally productive.

MULTIPLE-CHOICE QUESTIONS

38. _____ Derived demand refers to
   a. an individual's demand for a good from which he/she derives utility.
   b. an individual's demand for an input from which he/she derives utility.
   c. a firm's demand for a good from which it derives utility.
   d. a firm's demand for a input for the purpose of producing output.
   e. a and d.

39. _____ A firm's demand curve for an input is downward sloping because a lower input price will
   a. decrease demand for the firm's output.
   b. enable the firm to produce any given level of output more cheaply by using more of that input.
   c. typically cause the firm to use more of every input if the firm chooses to expand production.
   d. enable the firm to produce any given level of output more cheaply by using less of that input.
   e. b and c.

40. _____ Economic rent equals
     a. the actual payment made to an input.
     b. the minimum amount required to keep the input in its present use.
     c. the sum of the actual payment made to an input and the minimum amount required to keep the input in its present use.
     d. the difference between the actual payment made to an input and the minimum amount required to keep the input in its present use.
     e. the payments a tenant makes to his/her landlord.

41. _____ Graphically, economic rent can be illustrated by the area
     a. beneath the input's supply curve.
     b. beneath the input's demand curve.
     c. between the input's supply curve and its price.
     d. between the input's demand curve and its price.
     e. a and b.

42. _____ The magnitude of an input's economic rent depends on the
     a. demand elasticity of the good being produced.
     b. cross price elasticity of demand of the good being produced.
     c. demand elasticity of the input itself.
     d. supply elasticity of the input itself.
     e. a and b.

43. _____ As supply for an input becomes more inelastic, economic rent
     a. increases.
     b. decreases.
     c. remains the same.
     d. may increase, decrease, or remain the same.
     e. never increases.

44. _____ When the entire payment to an input is economic rent, its supply is
     a. elastic.
     b. unit elastic.
     c. inelastic, but not completely inelastic.
     d. completely inelastic.
     e. perfectly elastic.

45. _____ A firm's marginal revenue is defined as the
   a. change in the firm's total revenue resulting from the production of one additional unit of output.
   b. ratio of the firm's total revenue to output.
   c. change in the firm's total revenue resulting from the employment of one additional unit of the input.
   d. ratio of the firm's total revenue to the amount of input used.
   e. value of the additional output produced resulting from the employment of one additional unit of the input.

46. _____ A firm's marginal revenue product of an input is defined as the
   a. change in the firm's total revenue resulting from the production of one additional unit of output.
   b. ratio of the firm's total revenue to output.
   c. change in the firm's total revenue resulting from the employment of one additional unit of the input.
   d. ratio of the firm's total revenue to the amount of input used.
   e. value of the additional output produced resulting from the employment of one additional unit of the input.

47. _____ A firm's marginal revenue product of an input equals
   a. the firm's marginal revenue times the price of the input.
   b. the firm's marginal revenue times the input's marginal physical product.
   c. the price of the output times the input's marginal expense.
   d. the price of the input times the input's marginal physical product.
   e. b and c.

48. _____ A firm's marginal cost equals the
   a. change in the firm's total cost resulting from the production of one additional unit of output.
   b. ratio of the firm's total cost to output.
   c. change in the firm's total cost resulting from the employment of one additional unit of the input.
   d. ratio of the firm's total cost to the amount of input used.
   e. b and d.

49. _____ A firm's marginal expense of an input equals the
  a. change in the firm's total cost resulting from the production of one additional unit of output.
  b. ratio of the firm's total cost to output.
  c. change in the firm's total cost resulting from the employment of one additional unit of the input.
  d. ratio of the firm's total cost to the amount of input used.
  e. b and d.

50. _____ A profit-maximizing firm will hire an input until marginal revenue
  a. equals the input's marginal expense.
  b. product of the input equals the input's marginal expense.
  c. product of the input equals marginal cost.
  d. equals marginal cost.
  e. a and b.

51. _____ If a firm is a price taker in the input market, the input's marginal expense
  a. will be greater than the input's price.
  b. will be less than the input's price.
  c. will equal the input's price.
  d. may be greater than, less than, or equal to the input's price.
  e. will be less than marginal revenue.

52. _____ A firm's marginal value product of an input is defined as the
  a. change in the firm's total revenue resulting from the production of one additional unit of output.
  b. ratio of the firm's total revenue to output.
  c. change in the firm's total revenue resulting from the employment of one additional unit of the input.
  d. ratio of the firm's total revenue to the amount of input used.
  e. value of the additional output produced resulting from the employment of one additional unit of the input.

53. _____ The firm's marginal value product of an input equals
  a. the firm's marginal revenue times the price of the input.
  b. the firm's marginal revenue times the input's marginal expense.
  c. the price of the output times the input's marginal physical product.
  d. the price of the input times the input's marginal physical product.
  e. b and d.

54. _____ If a firm is a price taker in the output market, its marginal value product
    a. will be greater than its marginal revenue product.
    b. will be less than its marginal revenue product.
    c. will equal its marginal revenue product.
    d. may be greater than, less than, or equal to its marginal revenue product.
    e. will equal marginal revenue.

55. _____ A decrease in the price of an input leads to
    a. a substitution effect only.
    b. an income effect only.
    c. both a substitution and income effect.
    d. an output effect only.
    e. both a substitution and output effect.

56. _____ As a consequence of the substitution effect, a decrease in an input's price will cause a firm to use
    a. more of the input always.
    b. less of the input always.
    c. the same amount of the input always.
    d. less of the input, if the input is not inferior.
    e. the same amount of the input, if the input is not inferior.

57. _____ As a consequence of the output effect, a decrease in an input's price that leads to a downward shift of a firm's cost curves will cause the firm to use
    a. more of the input always.
    b. less of the input always.
    c. the same amount of the input always.
    d. more of the input, if the input is not inferior.
    e. less of the input, if the input is not inferior.

58. _____ The substitution effect will be large if
    a. it is easy for the firm to substitute for labor.
    b. it is difficult for the firm to substitute for labor.
    c. the demand for the good produced by the firm is elastic.
    d. the demand for the good produced by the firm is inelastic.
    e. the firm's marginal cost curve shifts little when the wage changes.

59. _____ The output effect will be small if
   a. it is easy for the firm to substitute for labor.
   b. it is difficult for the firm to substitute for labor.
   c. the demand for the good produced by the firm is elastic.
   d. the demand for the good produced by the firm is inelastic.
   e. the firm's marginal cost curve shifts little when the wage changes.

60. _____ If a firm is a monopoly in an output market, the firm is
   a. the only supplier of the input.
   b. the only supplier of the output.
   c. the only demander of the input.
   d. the only demander of the output.
   e. a and d.

61. _____ If a firm is a monopsonist in an input market, the firm is
   a. the only supplier of the input.
   b. the only supplier of the output.
   c. the only demander of the input.
   d. the only demander of the output.
   e. a and d.

62. _____ If a firm is a monopsonist in an input market, the input's marginal expense
   a. will be greater than the input's price.
   b. will be less than the input's price.
   c. will equal the input's price.
   d. may be greater than, less than, or equal to the input's price.
   e. is never greater than the input's price.

RUNNING GLOSSARY

63. _____ _____ demand: demand for a factor of production that is determined by the demand for the good it produces.

64. _____ Economic rent: the amount by which payments of a factor _____ the minimal amount required to retain it in its present use.

65. _____ Marginal revenue product: the extra revenue obtained from selling the output produced by hiring a(n) _____ worker or machine.

66. _____ Marginal value product: a special case of marginal revenue product in which the firm is a price taker for its _____.

67. _____ Substitution effect: in the theory of production, the substitution of one input for another while holding output _____ in response to a change in the input's price.

68. _____ Output effect: the change in the amount of an input that the firm hires that results from a change in the _____ level. Output changes because the change in an input's price affects the firm's costs.

69. _____ _____: a firm that is the only hirer in a particular input market.

70. _____ Marginal expense: the cost of hiring one more unit of the _____. Will exceed the price of the input if the firm faces an upward sloping supply curve for the input.

ANSWERS

1. equals	25. supply	49. c
2. labor	26. labor	50. b
3. cost	27. supply	51. c
4. times	28. higher	52. e
5. output	29. exceed	53. c
6. output	30. higher	54. c
7. output	31. wage	55. e
8. revenues	32. increase	56. a
9. revenues	33. wage	57. d
10. equals	34. exceed	58. a
11. labor	35. one	59. e
12. price	36. discriminate	60. b
13. equals	37. wages	61. c
14. price	38. d	62. a
15. expense	39. e	63. Derived
16. more	40. d	64. exceed
17. fall	41. c	65. extra
18. substitution	42. d	66. output
19. marginal	43. a	67. constant
20. inferior	44. d	68. output
21. output	45. a	69. Monopsony
22. substitute	46. c	70. input
23. large	47. b	
24. marginal	48. a	

APPENDIX TO CHAPTER 14

LABOR SUPPLY

LEARNING OBJECTIVES

- An individual decides on the quantity of labor he/she wishes to supply so as to maximize his/her utility.
- An increases in the wage rate has an ambiguous effect on labor supply. The substitution effect decreases leisure and increases labor supply; the income effect increases leisure and decreases labor supply.

WALKING TOUR SUMMARIES

ALLOCATION OF TIME

1. _____

2. _____

To purchase consumption goods, individuals must first earn _____. The more hours worked, the more income one earns. On the other hand, the more hours one works, the fewer hours of _____ one has to enjoy. Every individual faces a budget constraint that illustrates his tradeoff between consumption goods and leisure.

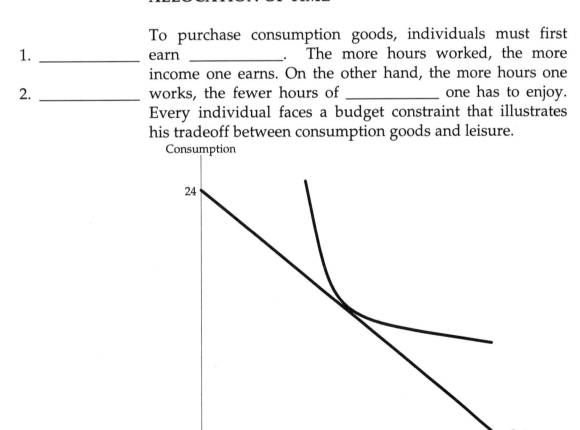

Figure 14a.1: *Utility-Maximizing Allocation of Time*

To understand what the budget constraint looks like, consider two extreme cases. If the individual consumes 24 hours of leisure a day, he/she earns no income and hence consumes no consumption goods. Therefore, the leisure

3. _____ intercept is _____. On the other hand, if the individual consumes no leisure, he/she would be working 24 hours a day. In this case, he/she can buy 24 × w dollars of consumption goods. Therefore, the

4. _____ _____ intercept is 24 × w. 24 and 24 × w are the two intercepts of the budget constraint. Graphing leisure on the horizontal axis and consumption goods on the vertical axis,

5. _____ the _____ of the budget constraint equals w. The individual will choose that bundle of consumption goods and leisure on his/her budget constraint that

6. _____ _____ his/her utility. The indifference curve passing through the individual's utility-maximizing bundle

7. _____ must be _____ to his/her budget constraint. Thus,

8. _____ his/her marginal rate of _____ will equal the wage rate.

INCOME AND SUBSTITUTION EFFECTS OF A CHANGE IN THE REAL WAGE RATE

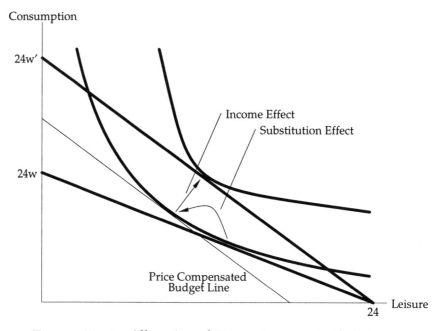

Figure 14a.2: *Allocation of Time – Increase in the Wage*

If the wage rate increases, the budget constraint shifts out by

9. _____ rotating about the 24-hour point on the _____ axis;

- 234 -

10. _____ the consumption good intercept _____ while the leisure intercept remains the same. Obviously, the individual can now achieve a higher level of utility. We can use income and substitution effects to describe what happens to his/her utility maximizing bundle. As a result

11. _____ of the substitution effect, the individual consumes _____ leisure. The income effect leads to the consumption of more

12. _____ leisure, however, because leisure is a(n) _____ good. The net effect on leisure depends on the relative magnitudes of the two effects. If the substitution effect dominates,

13. _____ higher wages lead to _____ leisure and consequently

14. _____ _____ work. The individual's supply curve for labor

15. _____ will be _____ sloping. On the other hand, if the income effect dominates, the individual's labor supply curve

16. _____ would be _____ sloping. We can construct the market labor supply curve by adding each individual's

17. _____ curve _____.

MULTIPLE-CHOICE QUESTIONS

18. _____ The more hours an individual works
    a. the more income he/she earns.
    b. the more consumption goods he/she can purchase.
    c. the more leisure he/she can enjoy.
    d. the less his/her wage rate becomes.
    e. a and b.

19. _____ An individual's "time use" budget constraint illustrates
    a. all the bundles of work and leisure that the individual can consume.
    b. all the bundles of consumption goods and leisure that the individual can consume.
    c. all the bundles of work and leisure that will keep the individual just as well off.
    d. all the bundles of consumption goods and leisure that keep the individual just as well off.
    e. c and d.

20. _____ For a given day, the leisure intercept of an individual's "time use" budget constraint is
   a. 24 hours.
   b. 24 times the individual's hourly wage.
   c. 24 divided by the individual's hourly wage.
   d. 365 times the individual's hourly wage.
   e. none of the above.

21. _____ For a given day, the consumption good intercept of an individual's "time use" budget constraint is
   a. 24 hours.
   b. the amount of consumption goods the individual could purchase with 24 times his/her wage rate of income.
   c. the amount of consumption goods the individual could purchase with 24 divided by his/her wage rate of income.
   d. the amount of consumption goods the individual could purchase with 365 times his/her wage rate of income.
   e. none of the above.

22. _____ For a given day with consumption goods on the vertical axis and leisure on the horizontal axis, the slope of an individual's "time use" budget constraint is the negative of
   a. his/her hourly wage rate.
   b. 1 divided by his/her hourly wage rate.
   c. 24 times his/her hourly wage rate.
   d. 24 divided by his/her hourly wage rate.
   e. b and d.

23. _____ An individual's "time use" indifference curve illustrates
   a. all the bundles of work and leisure that the individual can consume.
   b. all the bundles of consumption goods and leisure that the individual can consume.
   c. all the bundles of work and leisure that keep the individual just as well off.
   d. all the bundles of consumption goods and leisure that keep the individual just as well off.
   e. a and b.

24. _____ When an individual maximizes his/her utility,
   a. the indifference curve passing through his/her bundle must be tangent to the budget constraint.
   b. his marginal rate of substitution equals the wage.
   c. his marginal rate of substitution must equal the slope of the utility function.
   d. all bundles that he/she prefers must lie above the budget constraint.
   e. a, b, and d.

25. _____ Whenever the wage rate increases, the "time use" budget constraint shifts
   a. outward in a parallel fashion.
   b. inward in a parallel fashion.
   c. outward by rotating about the leisure intercept.
   d. outward by rotating about the consumption goods intercept.
   e. inward by rotating about the consumption goods intercept.

26. _____ An increase in the wage rate leads to
   a. an income effect only.
   b. a substitution effect only.
   c. both an income and a substitution effect.
   d. neither an income nor a substitution effect.
   e. an output effect.

27. _____ As a consequence of the substitution effect, an increase in the wage will lead to
   a. an increase in leisure.
   b. a decrease in leisure.
   c. an increase in consumption goods.
   d. a decrease in consumption goods.
   e. b and c.

28. _____ As a consequence of the income effect, an increase in the wage will lead to
   a. an increase in leisure always.
   b. a decrease in leisure always.
   c. an increase in leisure, if leisure is a normal good.
   d. a decrease in leisure, if leisure is an normal good.
   e. none of the above.

29. _____ If leisure were an inferior good, an increase in the wage will lead to
      a. an increase in leisure always.
      b. a decrease in leisure always.
      c. an increase in leisure only if the substitution effect dominates the income effect.
      d. an increase in leisure only if the income effect dominates the substitution effect.
      e. none of the above.

30. _____ If leisure is a normal good, an increase in the wage will lead to
      a. an increase in leisure always.
      b. a decrease in leisure always.
      c. an increase in leisure only if the substitution effect dominates the income effect.
      d. an increase in leisure only if the income effect dominates the substitution effect.
      e. none of the above.

31. _____ If leisure is a normal good, an increase in the wage will lead to
      a. an increase in hours worked always.
      b. a decrease in hours worked always.
      c. an increase in hours worked only if the substitution effect dominates the income effect.
      d. an increase in hours worked only if the income effect dominates the substitution effect.
      e. none of the above.

RUNNING GLOSSARY

32. _____ _____: time spent in any activity other than market work.

Substitution effect of a change in the wage: movement
33. _____ _____ an indifference curve in response to a change in the real wage. A rise in the wage causes an individual to
34. _____ work _____.

Income effect of a change in the wage: movement to a higher
35. _____ indifference curve in response to a(n) _____ in the real wage. If leisure is a normal good, a rise in the wage
36. _____ causes an individual to work _____.

ANSWERS

1. income
2. leisure
3. 24
4. consumption
5. slope
6. maximizes
7. tangent
8. substitution
9. leisure
10. increases
11. less
12. normal

13. less
14. more
15. upward
16. downward
17. horizontally
18. e
19. b
20. a
21. b
22. a
23. d
24. e

25. c
26. c
27. e
28. c
29. b
30. d
31. c
32. Leisure
33. along
34. more
35. rise
36. less

CHAPTER 15

TIME AND INTEREST RATES

LEARNING OBJECTIVES
- The interest rate is determined in the market for loanable funds; that is, the interest rate is determined by the demand and supply of loanable funds.
- When individuals save, they supply loanable funds.
- Firms demand loanable funds to invest in capital equipment.
- The present discounted value of a future payment equals what is needed at the present time to generate the payment in the future.

WALKING TOUR SUMMARIES

TIME PERIODS AND THE FLOW OF ECONOMIC TRANSACTIONS

1. _____ In economics, time plays an important role for both firms and consumers. First, some goods are _____, meaning that can be used for two or more periods. Automobiles, refrigerators, etc. are durable goods that are purchased by consumers. Most machines and equipment purchased by firms also operate for several years. Second, time plays a key role when individuals borrow or

2. _____ _____. For example, when an individual saves, he/she consumes less this year so that more can be consumed in the

3. _____ _____.

SUPPLY OF LOANABLE FUNDS - INDIVIDUAL SAVINGS

4. _____ When individuals save, they _____ loanable funds to the loanable funds market. We can use a two-period model to understand why individuals save. Let

C_0 = consumption this year
C_1 = consumption next year
r = interest rate

Suppose that an individual earns Y dollars of income this year and nothing next year. The individual must now consider alternatives. If the individual consumed all Y dollars this year, he/she would _____ nothing; consequently, since he/she earns no income next year, he/she would have nothing available to consume next year. To summarize, if the individual consumes all Y dollars of income this year, he/she would be consuming nothing next year; that is,

5. _____

$$C_0 = Y$$
$$C_1 = 0$$

Alternatively, if he/she consumed nothing this year, he/she would save _____ the Y dollars earned this year. Next year, he/she could consume the Y dollars earned this year plus the interest that Y dollars would earn. In one year, Y dollars would earn _____ of interest. Next year, the individual would have a total of Y + Yr available to spend. To summarize, if the individual consumed nothing this year, he/she would have _____ dollars available to spend next year; that is,

6. _____

7. _____

8. _____

$$C_0 = 0$$
$$C_1 = Y + Yr = Y(1 + r)$$

Fortunately, the individual need not choose one of these two extreme alternatives; he/she can choose alternates between these extremes. He/she could consume half the Y dollars this year and save the remaining half for next year or he/she could consumer two-thirds of the Y dollars this year and save the remaining one-third, etc. Figure 15.1 illustrates all the possible alternatives available to the individual by joining the points representing the two extreme alternatives with a(n) _____ line:

9. _____

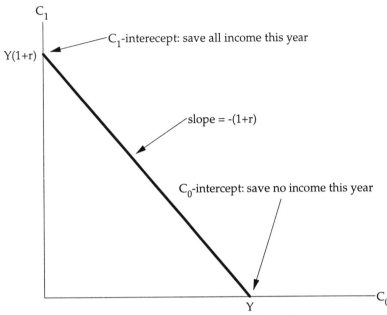

Figure 15.1: Two Period Budget Constraint

This straight line is the individual's budget line. The

10. _____ C_0-intercept of the budget line is _____; the C_1-intercept is

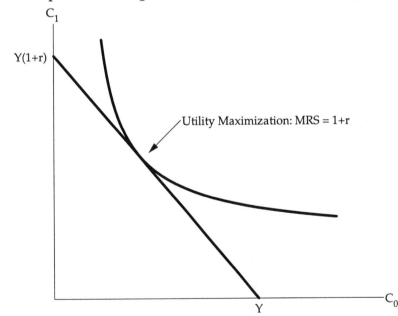

Figure 15.2: Two Period Utility Maximization

11. _____ $Y(1 + r)$. The slope of the budget line is _____. Which point on this budget line will he/she choose? The point which maximizes his/her utility; that is, the point at which the individual's marginal rate of substitution equals the

12. _____ negative of the slope of the _____ line:

- 243 -

13. _____   MRS = _____

What happens when the interest rate changes? Suppose that the interest rate increases. The C_0-intercept is

14. _____ unaffected while the C_1-intercept _____. The budget constraint rotates clockwise about the C_0-intercept. Both an income and substitution effects must now be considered. To

15. _____ illustrate these two effects, draw the price _____ budget line. As a consequence of the substitution effect,

16. _____ consumption this year falls and savings _____. As a consequence of the income effect, consumption this year

17. _____ rises and savings _____ (assuming that consumption

18. _____ this year is a(n) _____ good):

Substitution Effect   Income Effect
C_0 decreases C_0 increases
Savings increases   Saving decreases

The net effect of an interest rate rise depends on the relative magnitudes of the substitution and income effects.

19. _____ Economists generally believe that the _____ effect is larger. Consequently, an increase in the interest rate increases savings; therefore, the supply curve for loanable

20. _____ funds is _____ sloping.

DEMAND FOR LOANABLE FUNDS - FIRMS' DEMAND FOR CAPITAL

A profit-maximizing firm will use more equipment (capital) until the marginal revenue product of the equipment

21. _____ _____ the rental rate of the equipment. When

22. _____ the rental rate of capital is _____, a firm will demand little equipment; when the rental rate is low, the

23. _____ firm will demand _____ equipment. The interest rate

24. _____ affects the quantity of equipment _____ because the interest rate influences the rental rate of equipment. The rental rate includes two components: depreciation costs and borrowing costs:

Rental rate = Depreciation Costs + Borrowing Costs

25. _____ _____ costs reflect the physical wear and tear on equipment that occurs over the course of time. Borrowing costs may be either explicit or implicit. If the firm borrowed

funds to finance the purchase the equipment, borrowing

26. _____ costs are _____; on the other hand, if the firm used internal funds, implicit opportunity costs exist since the firm

27. _____ is _____ the interest that the funds would have earned. In either case, as the interest rate increases, the borrowing

28. _____ costs _____. Now, it is easy to understand how the interest rate influences the demand for loanable funds. When the interest rate falls, the rental rate decreases and

29. _____ firms seek to purchase _____ equipment. To do so, firms will demand more loans to finance the purchase of the equipment. Therefore, the demand curve for loanable funds

30. _____ is _____ sloping.

DETERMINATION OF THE REAL INTEREST RATE

It is easy to determine the equilibrium interest rate from the demand and supply curve for loanable funds. In

31. _____ equilibrium, the quantity demanded _____ the quantity supplied. Consequently, the intersection of the demand and supply curves in the loanable funds market illustrates the equilibrium interest rate.

PRESENT DISCOUNTED VALUE

32. _____ The present discounted value of _____ payable in one year equals the amount needed at the present time to generate \$1

a year from now. This just equals $\frac{1}{(1 + r)}$; it is easy to see

why. Place $\frac{1}{(1 + r)}$ dollars in a savings account; after one year, the balance will equal:

33. _____
$$\frac{1}{(1 + r)} \times (1 + r) = \underline{\quad}.$$
The present discounted value of \$1 payable in two years

34. _____ equals $\frac{1}{(1 + r)^2}$; that is, _____is needed at the present time to generate \$1 two years from now. To see why, place $\frac{1}{(1 + r)^2}$ in a savings account; after two years, the balance will equal:

$$\frac{1}{(1 + r)^2} \times (1 + r)^2 = \$1.$$

In general, the present discounted value of $D payable n years from now is $\frac{D}{(1 + r)^n}$. As the interest rate becomes larger, the present discounted value becomes smaller; as the interest rate becomes _____, less is required at the present time to generate $D in n years. As the payment moves further ahead in the future, the present discounted value of the payment becomes less. In a multi-period context, a firm's goal is to _____ the present discounted value of its profits.

35. _____

36. _____

PRICING OF EXHAUSTIBLE RESOURCES

Production of an exhaustible resource today reduces the amount that will be available in the _____. Thus, when a firm produces an exhaustible resource now, it will not be able to sell as much in the _____. Economists call this opportunity cost a(n) _____ cost. The magnitude of the scarcity cost depends on the expectation of future prices. If we believe that the price will rise rapidly, then the sale of the resource today will lead to a large _____ in future revenues. The scarcity cost would be _____. On the other hand, if we believe that the price will rise very slowly, the scarcity cost would be small.

37. _____

38. _____
39. _____

40. _____
41. _____

We estimate scarcity costs by comparing the price to _____ production costs. In a perfectly competitive industry, the price fully reflects all costs. Therefore, the scarcity costs would equal the difference between the price and marginal production costs.

42. _____

MULTIPLE-CHOICE QUESTIONS

43. _____ A durable good is a good that
   a. never goes out of style.
   b. lasts only one period.
   c. lasts at least five years.
   d. lasts for two or more periods.
   e. none of the above.

44. _____ Single period models cannot account for
   a. consumption.
   b. production.
   c. saving.
   d. borrowing.
   e. c and d.

45. _____ Consider a two-period model in which an individual earns Y dollars of income this year and earns nothing next year. The C_0-intercept of the individual's budget line equals
   a. Y.
   b. $Y(1 + r)$.
   c. $Y/(1 + r)$.
   d. $-(1 + r)$.
   e. $1/(1 + r)$.

46. _____ Consider a two-period model in which an individual earns Y dollars of income this year and earns nothing next year. The C_1-intercept of the individual's budget line equals
   a. Y.
   b. $Y(1 + r)$.
   c. $Y/(1 + r)$.
   d. $-(1 + r)$.
   e. $1/(1 + r)$.

47. _____ Consider a two-period model in which an individual earns Y dollars of income this year and earns nothing next year. The slope of the individual's budget line equals
   a. Y.
   b. $Y(1 + r)$.
   c. $Y/(1 + r)$.
   d. $-(1 + r)$.
   e. $1/(1 + r)$.

48. _____ Consider a two-period model in which an individual earns Y dollars of income this year and earns nothing next year. When the interest rate falls,
   a. the C_0-intercept of the individual's budget line decreases.
   b. the C_1-intercept of the individual's budget line decreases.
   c. the individual's budget line becomes more steep.
   d. a and b.
   e. none of the above.

49. _____ Consider a two-period model in which an individual earns Y dollars of income this year and earns nothing next year. When the interest rate rises,
   a. the C_0-intercept of the individual's budget line increases.
   b. the C_1-intercept of the individual's budget line increases.
   c. the individual's budget line becomes more steep.
   d. b and c.
   e. none of the above.

50. _____ In a two-period model, when an individual is maximizing his/her utility, his/her marginal rate of substitution equals
   a. $1/(1 + r)$.
   b. $(1 + r)$.
   c. $-1/(1 + r)$.
   d. $-(1 + r)$.
   e. none of the above.

51. _____ Consider a two-period model in which an individual earns Y dollars of income this year and earns nothing next year. When the interest rate rises, the substitution effect causes this year's consumption to
   a. always increase.
   b. always decrease.
   c. increase if this year's consumption is a normal good.
   d. decrease if this year's consumption is a normal good.
   e. none of the above.

52. _____ Consider a two-period model in which an individual earns Y dollars of income this year and earns nothing next year. When the interest rate rises, the substitution effect causes savings to
   a. always increase.
   b. always decrease.
   c. increase if this year's consumption is a normal good.
   d. decrease if this year's consumption is a normal good.
   e. none of the above.

53. _____ Consider a two-period model in which an individual earns Y dollars of income this year and earns nothing next year. When the interest rate rises, the income effect causes this year's consumption to
   a. always increase.
   b. always decrease.
   c. increase if this year's consumption is a normal good.
   d. decrease if this year's consumption is a normal good.
   e. none of the above.

54. _____ Consider a two-period model in which an individual earns Y dollars of income this year and earns nothing next year. When the interest rate rises, the income effect causes savings to
   a. always increase.
   b. always decrease.
   c. increase if this year's consumption is a normal good.
   d. decrease if this year's consumption is a normal good.
   e. none of the above.

55. _____ Most economists believe that when the interest rate changes,
   a. the substitution effect exceeds the income effect.
   b. the income effect exceeds the substitution effect.
   c. the income effect equals the substitution effect.
   d. the substitution effect is negligible.
   e. b and d.

56. _____ Most economists believe that the supply curve for loanable funds is
   a. upward sloping.
   b. downward sloping.
   c. vertical.
   d. horizontal.
   e. c or d.

57. _____ The rental rate of equipment (capital)
    a. includes borrowing costs only.
    b. equals the interest rate.
    c. includes depreciation costs only.
    d. include borrowing and depreciation costs.
    e. none of the above.

58. _____ When the interest rate increases,
    a. depreciation costs increase.
    b. depreciation costs decrease.
    c. borrowing costs increase.
    d. borrowing costs decrease.
    e. b and c.

59. _____ When the interest rate increases,
    a. rental rate of equipment decreases.
    b. rental rate of equipment increases.
    c. borrowing costs decrease.
    d. borrowing costs increase.
    e. b and d.

60. _____ The demand curve for loanable funds is
    a. upward sloping.
    b. downward sloping.
    c. vertical.
    d. horizontal.
    e. c or d.

61. _____ Assume that the interest rate is 10 percent. The present discounted value of a \$1,000 payment in two years is
    a. $1{,}000 + 2\times(1{,}000 \times .1) = 1{,}000 + 2\times100 = 1{,}200.$
    b. $1{,}000 \times (1 + .1)^2.$
    c. $\dfrac{1{,}000}{(1 + .1)^2}.$
    d. \$2,000.
    e. none of the above.

62. _____ When the interest rate falls, the present discounted value of a payment to be received in the future
    a. increases.
    b. decreases.
    c. is unchanged.
    d. a or c.
    e. none of the above.

63. _____ The production of an exhaustible resource at the present time
   a. increases the amount that can be produced in the future.
   b. decreases the amount that can be produced in the future.
   c. has no effect on the amount that can be produced in the future.
   d. may increase, decrease, or have no effect on the amount that can be produced in the future.
   e. decreases the amount that can be produced in the future only if the input is inferior.

64. _____ The scarcity cost is
   a. the out-of-pocket cost a firm incurs when producing an exhaustible resource at the present time.
   b. the accounting cost a firm incurs when producing an exhaustible resource at the present time.
   c. the opportunity cost a firm incurs when producing an exhaustible resource at the present time.
   d. the sum of the accounting and opportunity costs a firm incurs when producing an exhaustible resource at the present time.
   e. a and b.

65. _____ If a firm believes that the price of an exhaustible resource will rise rapidly in the future, scarcity cost
   a. will be low.
   b. will be high.
   c. will be unaffected.
   d. may be high, low, or unaffected.
   e. will be negative.

RUNNING GLOSSARY

66. _____ Durable: goods that last _____ or more periods.

67. _____ Supply of loanable funds reflect the _____ of individuals.

68. _____ _____ for loanable funds reflect the demand of firms for equipment (capital).

69. _____ Present discounted value of a future payment equals what is needed _____ in order to generate the future payment.

70. _____ _____ costs: the opportunity costs of forgone future production that cannot be made because of current production that uses exhaustible resources.

ANSWERS

1. durable
2. save
3. future
4. supply
5. save
6. all
7. Yr
8. $Y + Yr = Y(1 + r)$
9. straight
10. Y
11. $-(1 + r)$
12. budget
13. $1 + r$
14. increases
15. compensated
16. increases
17. decreases
18. normal
19. substitution
20. upward
21. equals
22. high
23. much
24. demanded

25. Depreciation
26. explicit
27. forgoing
28. increase
29. more
30. downward
31. equals
32. $1
33. 1
34. $1/(1 + r)^2$
35. larger
36. maximize
37. future
38. future
39. scarcity
40. decrease
41. high
42. current
43. d
44. e
45. a
46. b
47. d
48. b

49. d
50. b
51. b
52. a
53. c
54. d
55. a
56. a
57. d
58. c
59. e
60. b
61. c
62. a
63. b
64. c
65. b
66. two
67. savings
68. Demand
69. now
70. Scarcity

APPENDIX TO CHAPTER 15

COMPOUND INTEREST

LEARNING OBJECTIVES

- Interest is the payment a borrower must make for using someone else's funds for a period of time.
- Compound interest pays interest on the interest that was earned previously.
- Present discounted value of a payment to be received in the future equals what would be required at the present time to generate the future payment.
- In equilibrium, price of a machine equals its present discounted value.

WALKING TOUR SUMMARIES

INTEREST

1. _____
2. _____
3. _____
4. _____

Interest represents the _____ value of money. A borrower must pay _____ when he/she uses someone else's funds for a period of time. An individual borrows when he/she receives a(n) _____ from a bank. The amount of interest paid depends on the interest rate. For example, if the annual interest rate is 5 percent, a borrower must pay _____ for every $100 borrowed. On the other hand, when an individual saves by allowing someone else to use his/her funds for a time, interest is earned. An individual saves when he/she deposits funds in a saving account at a bank.

COMPOUND INTEREST

5. _____

6. _____

When an individual saves funds for more than one period, the interest is typically _____. This is true for the interest earned from a bank saving account. Suppose an individual saves $100. If the annual interest rate is 5 percent, the $100 will earn $5 of interest after one year:

Year 1 Interest = $100 × .05 = $5

and the savings account balance will equal _____:

$$\text{Balance after Year 1} = \$100 + 100 \times .05$$
$$\$100(1 + .05) = 105$$

During the second year, interest is earned on the entire

7. _____ _____ balance not on just the original $100:
$$\text{Year 2 interest} = \$105 \times .05 = \$5.25$$

8. _____ and the savings account balance will equal _____ after two years:

$$\text{Balance after Year 2} = \$105 + 5.25 = \$110.25$$
$$= \$105 + 105 \times .05$$
$$= \$105 (1 + .05)$$

But now recall that $105 = \$100(1 + .05)$:
$$\text{Balance after Year 2} = \$105 (1 + .05)$$
$$= \$100 (1 + .05)(1 + .05)$$
$$= \$100 (1 + .05)^2$$

We can generalize the notion of compound interest by letting the interest rate equal i; the balance that accumulates from saving D dollars for n years is:
$$\text{Balance after Year n} = D (1 + i)^n$$

PRESENT DISCOUNTED VALUE

The present discounted value of $1 payable in one year

9. _____ equals the amount needed at the _____ time to

10. _____ generate $1 a year from now. This just equals _____; it

is easy to see why. Place $\frac{1}{(1 + i)}$ dollars in a savings account; after one year, the balance will equal:

$$\frac{1}{(1 + i)} \times (1 + i) = \$1.$$

The present discounted value of $1 payable in two years

11. _____ equals _____; that is, $\frac{1}{(1 + i)^2}$ is needed at the present

time to generate $1 two years from now. To see why, place $\frac{1}{(1 + i)^2}$ in a savings account; after two years, the balance will equal:

$$\frac{1}{(1 + i)^2} \times (1 + i)^2 = \$1.$$

In general, the present discounted value of $D payable n years from now is $\frac{D}{(1 + i)^n}$. As the interest rate becomes larger the present discounted value becomes smaller; as the interest rate becomes larger, _____ is required at the present time to generate $D in n years. As the payment moves further ahead in the future, the present discounted value of the payment becomes _____.

12. _____

13. _____

DISCOUNTING PAYMENT STREAMS

14. _____

The present discounted value of an income stream equals the _____ of the present discounted values income received in each period. Consider a n year income stream. Let D_1 equal income received in one year; D_2 equal income received in two years; . . . D_n equal income received in n years. The present discounted value of this income stream is:

$$PDV = \frac{D_1}{(1 + i)} + \frac{D_2}{(1 + i)^2} + \cdots + \frac{D_n}{(1 + i)^n}$$

15. _____

A perpetuity provides a constant steam of payments _____. The present discounted value of a perpetuity which pays $D per year forever is $\frac{D}{i}$.

PRESENT DISCOUNTED VALUE APPROACH TO INVESTMENT DECISIONS

16. _____

Present discounted value provides an alternative way to explain the theory of investment. A machine provides the firm with a(n) _____ of net revenues in the future. Let R_1 equal the net revenues received in one year; R_2 equal the net revenues received in two years; . . . R_n equal the net revenues received in n years. Also, let r equal the rate of return the firm could earn from alternative investments. The machine's present discounted value is just:

$$PDV = \frac{R_1}{(1 + i)} + \frac{R_2}{(1 + i)^2} + \cdots + \frac{R_n}{(1 + i)^n}$$

17. _____

In equilibrium, the price of the machine must _____ the machine's present discounted value. If the price were _____ than the present discounted value, all firms

18. _____

would rush to buy the machine; there would be shortage of these machines leading to a higher price. If the price were greater than the present discounted value, no firm would purchase the machine; there would be a surplus leading to a

19. _____ _____ price.

The price of a machine and the rental rate of capital are related. For simplicity assume that machines do not
20. _____ depreciate. When the firm maximizes profit, the _____ rate of capital must equal the marginal revenue product:
$$MRP_K = v$$
Since the machine does not depreciate, the machine would bring the firm \$v of net revenue each year forever. This is a perpetuity:
$$PDV = \frac{v}{i}$$
In equilibrium, the price of the machine must equal its present discounted value:
$$P = \frac{v}{i}$$
Clearly,
$$v = iP.$$

MULTIPLE-CHOICE QUESTIONS

21. _____ In three years, \$1,000 earning a 10 percent compound interest rate will accumulate a balance of
   a. $1,000 + 3 \times (1,000 \times .1) = 1,000 + 3 \times 100 = 1,300$.
   b. $1,000 \times (1 + .1)^3$.
   c. $\dfrac{1,000}{(1 + .1)^3}$.
   d. \$3,000.
   e. none of the above.

22. _____ In three years, \$5,000 earning a 10 percent compound interest rate will accumulate a balance of
   a. $5,000 + 3 \times (5,000 \times .1) = 5,000 + 3 \times 500 = 6,500$.
   b. $5,000 \times (1 + .1)^3$.
   c. $\dfrac{5,000}{(1 + .1)^3}$.
   d. \$15,000.
   e. none of the above.

23. _____ Assume that the interest rate is 10 percent. The present discounted value of a $1,000 payment in three years is

    a. $1,000 + 3 \times (1,000 \times .1) = 10,00 + 3 \times 100 = 1,300$.

    b. $1,000 \times (1 + .1)^3$.

    c. $\dfrac{1,000}{(1 + .1)^3}$.

    d. $3,000.

    e. none of the above.

24. _____ When the interest rate rises, the present discounted value of a payment to be received in the future

    a. increases.

    b. decreases.

    c. is unchanged.

    d. a or c.

    e. none of the above.

25. _____ If the price of a machine were to exceed its present discounted value, the firm would

    a. purchase the machine only if the interest rate is less than the inflation rate.

    b. purchase the machine only if the interest rate exceeds the inflation rate.

    c. purchase the machine.

    d. not purchase the machine.

    e. none of the above.

26. _____ In equilibrium, the price of a machine must

    a. be greater than its present discounted value.

    b. be less than its present discounted value.

    c. equal its present discounted value.

    d. equal the rental rate of capital.

    e. none of the above.

RUNNING GLOSSARY

27. _____ _____ is payment for the current use of someone else's funds.

28. _____ Compound interest pays interest on the interest _____ earned.

29. _____ Present discounted value of a future payment equals what is needed now in order to generate the _____ payment.

30. _____ Perpetuity: a promise of a certain number of dollars each year, _____.

ANSWERS

1. time	11. $1/(1+i)^2$	21. b
2. interest	12. less	22. b
3. loan	13. less	23. c
4. $5	14. sum	24. b
5. compounded	15. forever	25. d
6. $105	16. stream	26. c
7. $105	17. equal	27. Interest
8. $110.25	18. less	28. previously
9. present	19. lower	29. future
10. $1/(1+i)$	20. rental	30. forever

CHAPTER 16

UNCERTAINTY AND INFORMATION

LEARNING OBJECTIVES

- Risk averse individuals refuse fair bets.
- Diminishing marginal utility of income explains why individuals are risk averse.
- Risk aversion explains why individuals purchase insurance and diversify their portfolios.
- There are both costs and benefits of obtaining information.

WALKING TOUR SUMMARIES

PROBABILITY AND EXPECTED VALUE

1. _____   The _____ of a particular outcome in a game is the relative frequency that the outcome would occur if the game were played many, many times. For example, when a coin is tossed, the probability of a head equals 1/2 (assuming of course that someone has not doctored the
2. _____   coin). The _____ value of a game with several uncertain prizes equals the size of the prize that the player will win on average. If the expected value of a game equals
3. _____   the cost of playing it, we call the game _____.

RISK AVERSION

4. _____   Individuals are typically risk _____; that is,
5. _____   individuals do not choose to participate in _____
6. _____   games. _____ marginal utility of income explains why individuals are risk averse. Although additional income always raises an individual's utility, the increase in utility resulting from equal increments of income becomes
7. _____   less and less as income _____. This means that while a fair game is fair in terms of dollars, it is not fair in terms of
8. _____   _____. Consider a game in which one wins $1,000 if a head appears on a coin toss, but loses $1,000 for a tail. The

Copyright © 2000 by Harcourt, Inc.

game is fair in terms of dollars, but not in terms of utility. In

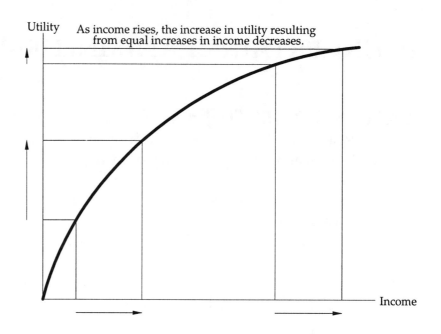

Figure 16.1: *Diminishing Marginal Utility of Income*

9. _____ terms of utility, the $1,000 loss brings _____ pain than the $1,000 win brings pleasure. Thus, risk

10. _____ _____ individuals refuse to play this game.

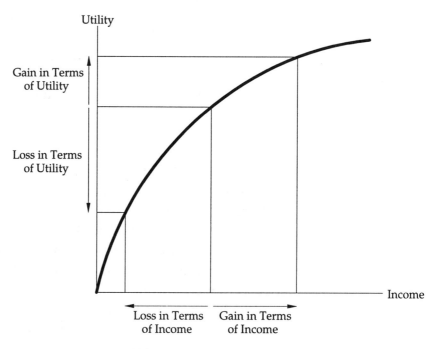

Figure 16.2: *Risk Aversion*

METHODS FOR REDUCING RISK

11. _____
12. _____
13. _____
14. _____
15. _____
16. _____
17. _____

Individuals purchase insurance to reduce risk. Because individuals are risk _____, they are willing to give up some income to avoid risk. An actuarially _____ insurance premium makes a risk-averse individual better off. In terms of income, the expected losses from the risky outcome would _____ the premium. In terms of utility, the expected pain of the risky losses would exceed the pain of paying the premium. Insurance companies must charge a premium _____ than the actuarially fair value to avoid losses, however. A risk-averse individual may or may not purchase such a policy. His actions depend on how risk averse he is and also by how much the actual premium exceeds the actuarially fair premium. Insurance companies do not offer policies to cover all types of risks; some are _____. Some types of risk are so rare and unpredictable that no one can estimate actuarially fair premiums. _____ selection can lead to uninsured risks when insurance companies and potential customers do not both have accurate assessments of the risks involved. _____ hazard can limit coverage when purchasing the policy affects the behavior of the policyholders.

18. _____
19. _____

Risk _____ individuals reduce risk by diversifying their assets. By not "_____ all your eggs in one basket," individuals increase their utility.

ECONOMICS OF INFORMATION

20. _____
21. _____

22. _____

All uncertain situations share one similar characteristic, the lack of complete _____. Individuals implicitly or explicitly _____ how much information to acquire. Information is similar to most economic goods in some respects, but is different in other ways. The decision concerning how much information to acquire is similar. Individuals weigh the benefits against the costs, as we do for goods. This explains why some individuals acquire more information than others. Some assess the benefits to be higher or the costs to be lower. Unlike most goods, however, it is often very difficult for an individual who has gathered information to prevent _____ from using it. Patent laws try to protect

23. _____

24. _____

25. _____

inventors by giving the exclusive rights to their inventions. These laws do not enable the inventor to garner _____ the benefits of his ideas, however. Information acquisition activities benefit not only the individual bearing the costs, but _____ also. Economists believe that financial markets react quickly to new information. The _____ markets hypothesis asserts that market prices accurately reflect all available information.

Economists often use a utility-maximizing model to understand how individuals behave when facing uncertainty. An individual is assumed to face two possible

26. _____

outcomes, two _____ of the world. In the graph below, C_1 represents consumption if state 1 results; C_2 consumption if state 2 results. Each point on the certainty line represents a situation in which consumption is the

27. _____

_____ regardless of the state of the world. That is, along the certainty line, there is no uncertainty; our individual's consumption is unaffected by the state of the world. Points not on the certainty line represent situations in which the amount of consumption depends on the state of the world. By purchasing insurance, an individual would

28. _____

move _____ the certainty line.

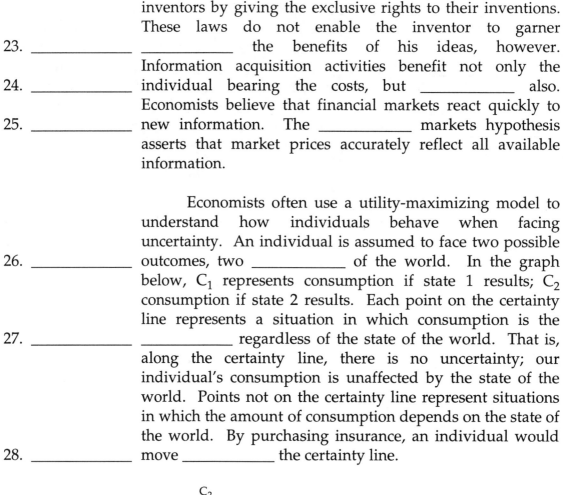

Figure 16.3: *Certainty Line and States of the World*

INFORMATION AND MARKET EQUILIBRIUM

While we know that an equilibrium price exists in every market, we have yet to describe a process that would lead the market to that price. In some markets an auctioneer serves this role. The _____ calls prices. Only when the quantity demanded _____ the quantity supplied will the transaction actually take place.

29. _____
30. _____

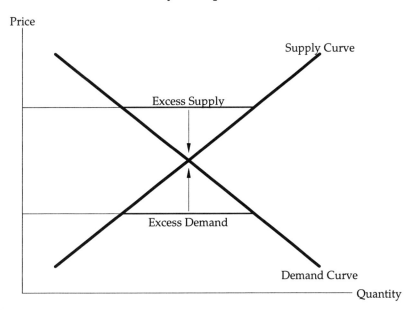

Figure 16.4: *Walrasian Price Adjustment*

31. _____
32. _____

Most markets do not employ actual auctioneers, however. Recontracting tries to circumvent this void. Buyers and sellers enter into _____ contracts that they complete only if price proves to be the _____ price. Otherwise, the parties negotiate new provisional contracts. After enough bargaining, the parties will achieve the equilibrium. Leon Walras proposed a second approach, which relies on the notion of excess _____. Excess demand equals the difference between the quantity demanded and the quantity supplied. The price increases whenever _____ demand is positive and decreases when excess demand is _____.

33. _____

34. _____
35. _____

36. _____
37. _____

While Walras views the _____ as the motivating force in the adjustment process, _____ relies on quantity instead. When the quantity is below the equilibrium level, individuals are willing to pay more for the good than its marginal cost. In this case, firms produce

- 267 -

38. _____ _____. Alternatively, when the quantity exceeds the
39. _____ equilibrium level, marginal cost _____ what
individuals are willing to pay and the quantity decreases.
Both Walras and Marshall achieve the same equilibrium
result, but the process responsible differs.

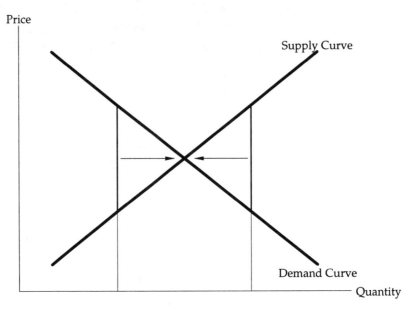

Figure 16.5: *Marshallian Price Adjustment*

Movement to an equilibrium typically involves
changes in both price and quantity. Economists explain
why demanders and sellers do not adjust instantaneously to
40. _____ the equilibrium by recognizing that _____ costs exist.
Demanders must discover where they can buy a particular
good and also must invest time in learning about the market
prices. Suppliers face similar costs. They must learn about
the demand for their product. Typically they react to the
short-run random nature of demand by maintaining
41. _____ _____. These transaction costs prevent the price and
quantity from adjusting to the equilibrium immediately.
Therefore, economists have studied the disequilibrium
behavior of prices.

MODELS OF DISEQUILIBRIUM PRICING

The cobweb model of price adjustment assumes that
suppliers base this period's production decisions on the
42. _____ _____ period's price. Suppliers expect that the
current period's price will equal last period's and decide on
their levels of production accordingly. After producing the

- 268 -

good, suppliers sell the output for what the market will bear. This process can result in a stable or unstable equilibrium. In the stable case, the price moves

43. _____ _____ the equilibrium. In the unstable case, the
44. _____ price moves away from the _____. The rational expectations model recognizes that demanders and suppliers typically base their price expectations on more
45. _____ than last period's price. With enough _____, parties all could calculate the equilibrium price precisely. Buyers and sellers would make their decisions on the actual equilibrium price. The quantity of information required for these calculations is considerable, however. Typically buyers and sellers base their expectations on incomplete
46. _____ _____.

INFORMATION AND ECONOMIC EFFICIENCY

Our proof that competitive markets lead to efficiency implicitly assumed that all economic actors are
47. _____ _____ informed. Without full information, competitive markets can result in inefficiency. Asymmetric information on the part of the buyer and seller can lead to such a result. For example, the seller of a used car has more information about the quality of the automobile than the
48. _____ buyer. The _____ problem can arise. Buyers and sellers will trade fewer used cars than efficiency dictates.
49. _____ This is an example of _____ selection. Adverse selection occurs whenever one party has more information than others. The party possessing the most information enjoys an advantage in the marketplace. Adverse selection can occur in a wide variety of markets: insurance, labor, etc. Competitive markets provide buyers and sellers with
50. _____ incentives to acquire _____. The ramifications of this are complex, however, and economists have been unable to draw many general conclusions.

MULTIPLE-CHOICE QUESTIONS

51. _____ The probability of an event is
    a. the relative frequency with which the outcome would occur.
    b. what a player would win on average if a game were played many, many times.
    c. what a player can be assured of winning if he plays a game once.
    d. what a player can be assured of losing if he plays a game once.
    e. the difference between c and d.

52. _____ The expected value of a game is
    a. the relative frequency that each outcome would occur if the game were played many, many times.
    b. what a player would win on average if the game were played many, many times.
    c. what a player can be assured of winning if he plays the game once.
    d. what a player can be assured of losing if he plays the game once.
    e. the difference between c and d.

53. _____ If a game is fair, the cost of playing the game
    a. is greater than its expected value.
    b. is less than its expected value.
    c. equals its expected value.
    d. is unrelated to its expected value.
    e. equals its expected value times the probability of winning.

54. _____ Individuals are
    a. usually risk averse.
    b. usually risk takers.
    c. usually risk neutral.
    d. always risk neutral.
    e. never risk averse.

55. _____ A risk-averse individual will
    a. want to play a fair game.
    b. not want to play a fair game.
    c. be indifferent about playing a fair game.
    d. be undecided about playing a fair game.
    e. always gamble at the race track.

56. _____ Risk aversion can be explained by
    a. increasing marginal utility of income.
    b. decreasing marginal utility of income.
    c. constant marginal utility of income.
    d. constant marginal rate of substitution.
    e. b and d.

57. _____ If an individual is a risk averter
    a. a $1,000 loss brings more pain than a $1,000 gain brings pleasure.
    b. a $1,000 gain brings more pleasure than a $1,000 loss brings pain.
    c. a $1,000 loss brings just as much pain as a $1,000 gain brings pleasure.
    d. his marginal rate of substitution is constant.
    e. his marginal utility of income is increasing.

58. _____ A risk may be uninsurable if insurance would lead to
    a. adverse selection.
    b. moral hazard.
    c. a premium which is more than fair.
    d. a and b.
    e. a and c.

59. _____ Information is similar to most goods in that
    a. all the benefits enjoyed by acquiring information are enjoyed by the individual who incurs the cost of acquiring it.
    b. some of the benefits enjoyed by acquiring information are not enjoyed by the individual who incurs the cost of acquiring it.
    c. individuals decide to acquire information whenever the benefits exceed the costs.
    d. individuals decide to acquire information whenever the benefits are positive.
    e. a and c.

60. _____ Information is dissimilar from most goods in that
   a. all the benefits enjoyed by acquiring information are enjoyed by the individual who incurs the cost of acquiring it.
   b. some of the benefits enjoyed by acquiring information are not enjoyed by the individual who incurs the cost of acquiring it.
   c. individuals decide to acquire information whenever the benefits exceed the costs.
   d. individuals decide to acquire information whenever the benefits are positive.
   e. a and c.

61. _____ An impartial auctioneer finds the equilibrium price by
   a. precise calculations involving demand and supply.
   b. calling out a single price.
   c. calling out successive prices until one is found at which quantity demanded equals quantity supplied.
   d. call out successive prices until one is found at which excess demand equals zero.
   e. c and d.

62. _____ Recontracting has been mentioned as a
   a. substitute for the impartial auctioneer when a market has none.
   b. way to increase the income of lawyers.
   c. way to reduce a firm's risks.
   d. way to find an equilibrium price.
   e. a and d.

63. _____ Excess demand equals the
   a. quantity demanded plus the quantity supplied.
   b. amount consumers would like to purchase if the market were in equilibrium.
   c. difference between the value consumers place on the consumption of a good and what they must pay to purchase the good.
   d. sum of consumers' surplus and profit.
   e. none of the above.

64. _____ Walras argues that an equilibrium will be achieved by
    a. an increase (decrease) in the price whenever excess demand is positive (negative).
    b. a decrease (increase) in the price whenever excess demand is positive (negative).
    c. an increase (decrease) in the quantity whenever the price exceeds marginal cost.
    d. a decrease (increase) in the quantity whenever the price exceeds (falls short of) marginal cost.
    e. a and c.

65. _____ Marshall argues that an equilibrium will be achieved by
    a. an increase (decrease) in the price whenever excess demand is positive (negative).
    b. a decrease (increase) in the price whenever excess demand is positive (negative).
    c. an increase (decrease) in the quantity whenever the price exceeds marginal cost.
    d. a decrease (increase) in the quantity whenever the price exceeds (falls short of) marginal cost.
    e. b and d.

66. _____ Transaction costs explain why
    a. a market must always be in disequilibrium.
    b. a market must always be in equilibrium.
    c. the quantity demanded equals the quantity supplied.
    d. the length of time during which a market is in disequilibrium varies from market to market.
    e. none of the above.

67. _____ The cobweb model assumes that
    a. demanders base their consumption decisions on last period's price.
    b. suppliers base their production decisions on last period's price.
    c. demanders base their consumption decisions on this period's price.
    d. b and c.
    e. a and b.

68. _____ The cobweb model predicts that
     a. all markets will be stable.
     b. all markets will be unstable.
     c. some markets will have a stable price, but an unstable quantity.
     d. some markets will have an unstable price, but a stable quantity.
     e. none of the above.

69. _____ Rational expectations argues that
     a. the cobweb model is over simplistic.
     b. with complete information individuals would be able to calculate the equilibrium price.
     c. all individuals know about elasticities.
     d. prices should never change.
     e. none of the above.

70. _____ Asymmetric information
     a. explains why colleges admit some students who do not graduate.
     b. explains why the "lemons" problem exists.
     c. occurs whenever all individuals are not fully informed.
     d. occurs only if all individuals are fully informed.
     e. none of the above.

71. _____ Adverse selection
     a. may occur when buyers and sellers have different information.
     b. may occur when there is asymmetric information.
     c. may lead to inefficiency.
     d. helps those groups who have better information.
     e. all of the above.

72. _____ Models attempting to capture the acquisition of information
     a. yield many general and far reaching results.
     b. suggest that market equilibrium is complex in this context.
     c. indicate that efficiency always results if there is asymmetric information.
     d. suggest that information can be acquired costlessly.
     e. none of the above.

RUNNING GLOSSARY

73. _____ _____: the relative frequency with which an event occurs.

74. _____ Expected value: the _____ outcome from an uncertain gamble.

75. _____ Fair games: games that cost their _____ value.

76. _____ Risk aversion: the tendency of people to refuse to accept _____ games.

77. _____ _____ insurance: insurance for which the premium is equal to the expected value of the loss.

78. _____ Averse selection: the possibility that individuals know more about their expected _____ than do insurers (or other market participants).

79. _____ _____ hazard: the effect that having insurance has on the behavior of the insured.

80. _____ _____: the spreading of risk among several options rather than choosing only one.

81. _____ Efficient markets hypothesis: the hypothesis that all information is reflected in prevailing market _____.

82. _____ _____ demand: the extent to which quantity demanded exceeds quantity supplied at a particular price.

83. _____ _____ costs: costs involved in making market transactions and in gathering information with which to make those transactions.

84. _____ Cobweb model: a model of price adjustment in which some trading takes place at _____ prices.

85. _____ Stable equilibrium: a situation in which market forces cause price to move _____ its equilibrium level.

86. _____ Unstable equilibrium: a situation in which market forces cause price to move _____ its equilibrium level.

87. _____ Rational expectations: basing price expectations on _____ information about the equilibrium price determined by the interaction of supply and demand in the market.

88. _____ Asymmetric information: a situation in which buyers and sellers have _____ amounts of information about a market transaction.

89. _____ _____ selection: when buyers and sellers have different information, market outcomes may exhibit adverse selection--the quality of goods or services traded will be biased toward market participants with better information.

ANSWERS

1. probability	31. provisional	61. e
2. expected	32. equilibrium	62. e
3. fair	33. demand	63. e
4. averse	34. excess	64. a
5. fair	35. negative	65. c
6. Diminishing	36. price	66. d
7. rises	37. Marshall	67. d
8. utility	38. more	68. e
9. more	39. exceeds	69. b
10. averse	40. transaction	70. b
11. averse	41. inventories	71. e
12. fair	42. previous	72. b
13. equal	43. toward	73. Probability
14. greater	44. equilibrium	74. average
15. uninsurable	45. information	75. expected
16. Averse	46. information	76. fair
17. Moral	47. fully	77. Fair
18. averse	48. lemon	78. losses
19. putting	49. adverse	79. Moral
20. information	50. information	80. Diversification
21. decide	51. a	81. prices
22. others	52. b	82. Excess
23. all	53. c	83. Transaction
24. others	54. a	84. nonequilibrium
25. efficient	55. b	85. to
26. states	56. b	86. from
27. same	57. a	87. complete
28. toward	58. d	88. different
29. auctioneer	59. c	89. Adverse
30. equals	60. b	

CHAPTER 17

EXTERNALITIES AND PUBLIC GOODS

LEARNING OBJECTIVES

- Coase Theorem: When property rights are assigned and bargaining costs are low, government intervention need not be necessary to cope with an externality. In these cases, bargaining leads to efficiency; the assignment of property rights does not effect how resources are ultimately allocated.
- When bargaining costs are substantial, government intervention may be needed to achieve efficiency. Traditionally, taxes and regulation have been suggested for these cases.
- Pure public goods have two distinguishing characteristics: nonexclusivity and nonrivalry.
- Inefficient provision of public goods result from their nonrival nature; the nonexclusive nature of public goods leads to the free rider problem.

WALKING TOUR SUMMARIES

DEFINING EXTERNALITIES

1. _____ An externality occurs whenever the price system does not account for an action undertaken by one economic actor that directly affects the well-being of _____ actor.

EXTERNALITIES, MARKETS, AND ALLOCATIONAL EFFICIENCY

Consider two firms, one producing eyeglasses and one charcoal. The charcoal firm pollutes the atmosphere whenever it produces charcoal. These pollutants damage the grinding instruments used by the eyeglass firm. Of course the production of eyeglasses depends on the inputs hired by the eyeglass firm. Eyeglass production also depends on the charcoal firm's level of production, however. When the charcoal firm increases production, it emits more pollutants causing more damage to the eyeglass

2. _____ firm. The pollution represents a(n) _____. The price system does not account for the harm that the charcoal firm inflicts upon the eyeglass firm. Inefficiency results because

3. _____ the charcoal firm's _____ costs are not equal to its social costs. The charcoal firm does not account for the damages done by its pollution; its private marginal cost

4. _____ curve lies _____ its social marginal cost curve. The difference in height represents the damage done by the pollutants. Since efficiency requires production to occur

5. _____ where price equals marginal _____ cost, the charcoal firm produces too much charcoal.

PROPERTY RIGHTS, BARGAINING, AND THE COASE THEOREM

Property rights refer to the legal specification of who owns a good. Furthermore, property rights may restrict the types of trades that the owner is allowed to make with

6. _____ others. Society at large owns _____ property. Therefore anyone can use it. Specific individuals own

7. _____ _____ property. Private property may be exchangeable or nonexchangeable.

If bargaining were costless in our charcoal-eyeglass externality example and if the air were made exchangeable

8. _____ private property, bargaining would lead to _____. The efficient outcome would occur regardless of which firm received the property right. If the charcoal firm received the right, the eyeglass firm would bribe the charcoal firm to reduce air pollutants. On the other hand, if the eyeglass firm received the right, the charcoal firm would pay for the right to pollute the air. While the assignment of

9. _____ _____ rights will not affect the allocation of

10. _____ resources, it will have a(n) _____ impact. If the charcoal firm receives the property right, it would receive a payment (from the eyeglass firm). Alternatively, if the eyeglass firm receives the right, the charcoal firm would make a payment (to the eyeglass firm).

11. _____ If bargaining were not costless, _____ would typically result, however. Environmental externalities

12. _____ usually involve _____ bargaining costs. For example, air pollution in an urban area affects the well-

13. _____ being of _____ individuals. It is frequently difficult,

14. _____ if not impossible, to organize these individuals into an effective bargaining unit. Furthermore, how can the affected parties calculate the monetary value of the losses suffered. When bargaining costs are _____, the assignment of property rights does affect the allocation of resources.

OTHER WAYS OF COPING WITH EXTERNALITIES

15. _____ Economists have long advocated the use of taxes to deal with externalities. The government could impose an excise tax on the charcoal firm. If the tax equaled the difference between the private and _____ marginal costs, the charcoal firm would reduce production to the efficient level. Also, the two firms could merge. The single firm would recognize the detrimental effect that charcoal production has on its glass grinding equipment. The firm would include this injurious effect in its marginal private cost curve of charcoal production. Consequently, the

16. _____ single firm would _____ the production of charcoal.
17. _____ Both taxes and mergers are traditional way to _____ the externality.

PUBLIC GOODS

18. _____ The most common definition of public goods stresses two aspects: nonexclusivity and nonrivalry. Exclusivity refers to whether an individual can be _____ from the benefits of a good, once the good is produced. A hamburger is exclusive, whereas national defense is not. Rivalry refers to the costs of extending the benefits to an

19. _____ _____ individual. A hamburger is rival, whereas a bridge at an off-peak hour is not.

20. _____ Private markets tend to produce an inefficiently _____ level of public goods. Each consumer in making his decision about whether or not to purchase a good only considers the benefits that will accrue to him individually. In the case of public goods this means that the potential buyer will not take into account the benefits that

21. _____ others enjoy. Since each consumer _____ the full social benefits involved, too little of a public good will be produced in a private market.

22. _____   As Lindahl demonstrates, _____ provision of a public good requires information regarding each individual's demand for the good. As a consequence of

23. _____ nonexclusivity, however, a(n) _____ rider problem arises whenever one attempts to collect this information. Each individual has an incentive to misrepresent his true

24. _____ preference regarding the _____ good.

LOCAL PUBLIC GOODS

Some economists suggest that a market-like mechanism exists for providing those public goods whose benefits

25. _____ are confined to a(n) _____ rather than national level. Just as individuals "vote with their dollars" to express their preferences in a market for private goods, individuals may "vote with their feet" to express their preferences by choosing their community of residence.

DIRECT VOTING AND RESOURCE ALLOCATION

If preferences are single-peaked, majority rule will result

26. _____ in the adoption of the _____ voter's most favored choice. Unfortunately, since many issues of public choice are multidimensional, preferences are typically not single peaked. In such cases, a voting equilibrium need not exist; every proposal may be defeated by some other proposal.

ANALYSIS OF REPRESENTATIVE GOVERNMENT

27. _____ _____ argues that parties in a representative democracy will behave in ways similar to firms in an

28. _____ economy. A party will seek to _____ its political support; it will pursue policies up to the point at which the marginal gain in votes from those individuals who benefit

29. _____ from the policy _____ the marginal loss in votes from those who are hurt.

30. _____ _____ describes the process of representative democracy quite differently by focusing on the role played

31. _____ by special interest groups. _____ contends that in a pluralistic society a systematic bias exists concerning the kinds of pressure groups that will develop. He contends that only those groups that represent narrow special

32. _____

interests will arise. In these close-knit groups each member recognizes the benefits of _____ action. Groups representing the broad public interest (that is the interests of a large number of individuals) will not develop as a

33. _____

consequence of the _____ rider problem, however.

34. _____

These two views of representative democracy can be combined by recognizing the _____ constraint. Special interest groups no doubt play a major role in the process, but politicians still must be concerned with pursuing policies that obtain the support of a(n)

35. _____ _____ of their electorate.

MULTIPLE-CHOICE QUESTIONS

36. _____ An externality causes competitive markets to be inefficient because
   a. one economic actor's well-being is affected by another in a way that is not taken into account by the normal operations of the market system.
   b. the market system does not make an economic actor aware of the full social consequences of his actions.
   c. consumers are public spirited.
   d. a and b.
   e. a and c.

37. _____ Economists have advocated which of the following "solutions" to the externality problem?
   a. forcing the firm producing the externality to shut down
   b. placing a tax on the economic activity that produces the externality
   c. prohibiting the activity associated with the externality
   d. a, b, and c
   e. a and b

38. _____ Property rights
   a. specify who owns a good.
   b. can never be bought and/or sold.
   c. for a particular good are always owned by a single person.
   d. specify the types of trades the owner of a good can make with others.
   e. a and d.

39. _____ Private property
     a. is owned by society at large.
     b. must be exchangeable.
     c. must by nonexchangeable.
     d. is owned by one specific person or group.
     e. c and d.

40. _____ If bargaining were costless, the assignment of private exchangeable property rights for an externality would
     a. guarantee efficiency.
     b. guarantee inefficiency.
     c. always have no effect.
     d. none of the above.
     e. b and c.

41. _____ If bargaining were costless, exactly who received the property rights for an externality would
     a. influence the allocation of resources.
     b. not influence the allocation of resources.
     c. not have a distributional impact.
     d. a and c.
     e. b and c.

42. _____ If bargaining were costly, exactly who received the property rights for an externality would
     a. influence the allocation of resources.
     b. not influence the allocation of resources.
     c. have a distributional impact.
     d. not have a distributional impact.
     e. a and c.

43. _____ Common property
     a. is owned by society at large.
     b. can be used by anyone with a direct charge.
     c. is owned by a small group of individuals.
     d. is owned by one specific group of people.
     e. a and b.

44. _____ The exclusive aspect of a good indicates
    a. how much it costs to extend the benefits of the good to an additional person.
    b. whether an individual can be excluded from consuming the benefits of a good once the good has been produced.
    c. whether the good is produced in a competitive industry.
    d. whether the good is sold by exclusive shops.
    e. a and b.

45. _____ The rivalry aspect of a good indicates
    a. how much it costs to extend the benefits of the good to an additional person.
    b. whether an individual can be excluded from consuming the benefits of a good once the good has been produced.
    c. whether the good is produced in a competitive industry.
    d. whether the good is sold by exclusive shops.
    e. b and c.

46. _____ Pure public goods are
    a. rival.
    b. nonrival.
    c. nonexclusive.
    d. a and c.
    e. b and c.

47. _____ Private markets produce
    a. an efficient level of pure public goods always.
    b. an inefficiently low level of pure public goods always.
    c. an inefficiently high level of pure public goods always.
    d. a level of pure public goods that may be greater than, less than, or equal to the efficient level.
    e. an efficient level of pure public goods when they are normal goods.

48. _____ Private markets produce an inefficiently low level of pure public goods because each individual in making his decision to purchase the good considers the benefits accruing to
    a. all society.
    b. the entire community.
    c. himself.
    d. the entire state.
    e. b and d.

49. _____ With a pure public good the free rider problem arises because
   a. of the good's nonexclusivity.
   b. of the good's nonrivalry.
   c. each individual has an incentive to misrepresent his preferences for the good.
   d. of the good's rivalry.
   e. a and c.

50. _____ If voter preferences are single peaked, majority rule results in
   a. no clear cut choice.
   b. the choice of the average voter.
   c. the choice of the median voter.
   d. a deadlock.
   e. a and d.

51. _____ Downs argues that in a representative democracy political parties will
   a. seek to maximize their political support.
   b. pursue policies up to the point at which the marginal gain in votes from individuals who benefit from the policy equals the marginal loss from those who are hurt.
   c. represent the broad public interest.
   d. represent the interests of narrow special concerns.
   e. a and b.

52. _____ Olson argues that in a representative democracy the special interest groups which develop will
   a. seek to maximize their political support.
   b. pursue policies up to the point at which the marginal gain in votes from individuals who benefit from the policy equals the marginal loss from those who are hurt.
   c. represent the broad public interest.
   d. represent the interests of narrow special concerns.
   e. a and c.

RUNNING GLOSSARY

53. _____   Externality: the effect of one party's economic activities on _____ party that is not taken into account by the price system.

54. _____   _____ costs: costs of production that include both input costs and costs of the externalities that production may cause.

55. _____   Pigovian tax: a tax or subsidy on an externality that brings about an equality of private and _____ marginal costs.

56. _____   _____ of an externality: incorporation of the social marginal costs of an externality into an economic actor's decision (as through taxation or merger).

57. _____   Property rights: the legal specification of who owns a good and the trades the _____ is allowed to make with it.

58. _____   Common property: property that may be used by _____ without cost.

59. _____   _____ property: property that is owned by specific people who may prevent others from using it.

60. _____   Coase theorem: if bargaining is _____, the social cost of an externality will be taken into account by the parties, and the allocation of resources will be the same no matter how property rights are assigned.

61. _____   _____ goods: goods that provide benefits that no one can be excluded from enjoying.

62. _____   Nonrival goods: goods that additional consumers may use at _____ marginal costs.

63. _____   _____ goods: goods that are both nonexclusive and nonrival.

64. _____   Lindahl equilibrium: balance between people's demand for public goods and the _____ shares that each must pay for them.

65. _____ Free rider: a consumer of a nonexclusive good who does not pay for it in the hope that _____ consumers will.

66. _____ _____ voter: a voter whose preferences for a public good represent the middle point of all voters' preferences for the good.

67. _____ _____ Rent-seeking behavior: firms or individuals influencing _____ policy to increase their own welfare.

ANSWERS

1. another
2. externality
3. private
4. below
5. social
6. common
7. private
8. efficiency
9. property
10. distributional
11. inefficiency
12. high
13. many
14. high
15. social
16. reduce
17. internalize
18. excluded
19. additional
20. low
21. underestimates
22. efficient
23. free

24. public
25. local
26. median
27. Downs
28. maximize
29. equals
30. Pluralism
31. Olson
32. collective
33. free
34. reelection
35. majority
36. d
37. b
38. e
39. d
40. a
41. b
42. e
43. a
44. b
45. a
46. e

47. b
48. c
49. e
50. c
51. e
52. d
53. another
54. Social
55. social
56. Internalization
57. owner
58. anyone
59. Private
60. costless
61. Nonexclusive
62. zero
63. Public
64. tax
65. other
66. Median
67. government

PART 5

FURTHER TOPICS

WALKING TOUR PROBLEMS

SUBSTITUTION AND OUTPUT EFFECTS

1. Initially, the wage rate of labor is $5.00 and the rental rate of capital is $10.00. The firm is producing 1,000 units of output. The wage rate increases from $5.00 to $7.50. Labor and capital are normal inputs.

   a. What happens to the slope of the firm's equal cost curve?

   The slope of the firm's equal cost curve is determined by the wage-rental ratio; it is the negative of the wage rate divided by the rental rate. Since the wage rate has risen, the equal costs curve has become _____ steeply sloped.

1. _____

   The answer is it becomes more steeply sloped.

   b. As a consequence of the substitution effect, what has happened to the cost-minimizing combination of labor and capital?

   The substitution effect indicates how the firm's choice of inputs would be affected, if it were to keep the level of output constant. Because labor has become more _____ relative to capital, the firm would substitute capital for labor if it wanted to produce the same level of output.

2. _____

   The answer is there is less labor and more capital.

   c. Typically what happens to the firm's marginal cost curve? To its profit-maximizing level of output?

3. _____

Since the cost of an input has increased, the marginal cost curve typically shifts _____.

The answer is it shifts up.

4. _____

Since the marginal cost curve has shifted up, the profit-maximizing level of output _____.

The answer is it decreases.

d. As a consequence of the output effect, what happens to the cost-minimizing combination of capital and labor?

5. _____
6. _____

7. _____
8. _____

9. _____

The output effect indicates how the firm's choice of inputs are affected by the _____ in the level of production. The level of output has _____. If an input is normal when the level of output decreases, the firm uses _____; on the other hand if an input is _____ when the level of output decreases, the firm uses more. Since both labor and capital are normal, the usage of each will _____ as a consequence of the output effect.

The answer is both decrease.

e. Accounting for both the substitution and output effects, what happens to the usage of labor and capital?

10. _____

For labor, the substitution and output effects work in the same direction causing the amount of labor used to _____ unambiguously. With capital the substitution effect leads to more usage, but the output effect leads to less; the total effect is uncertain.

The answer is less labor is used and there is an ambiguous effect on capital.

2. Initially, the wage rate of labor is $5.00 and the rental rate of capital is $10.00. The firm is producing 1,000 units of output. The wage rate increases from $5.00 to $7.50. Labor is a normal input; capital is inferior.

a. What happens to the slope of the firm's equal cost curve?

The slope of the firm's equal cost curve is determined by the wage-rental ratio; it is the _____ of the wage rate divided by the rental rate. Since the wage rate has risen, the equal costs curve has become _____ steeply sloped.

The answer is it becomes more steeply sloped.

11. _____

12. _____

b. As a consequence of the substitution effect, what has happened to the cost-minimizing combination of labor and capital?

The substitution effect indicates how the firm's choice of inputs would be affected if it were to keep the level of output _____. Because labor has become more expensive relative to capital, the firm would substitute _____ for labor if it wanted to produce the same level of output.

The answer is there is less labor and more capital.

13. _____

14. _____

c. Typically what happens to the firm's marginal cost curve? To its profit-maximizing level of output?

Since the cost of an input has increased, the marginal costs curve typically shifts up.

The answer is it shifts up.

Since the marginal cost curve has shifted _____, the profit-maximizing level of output has decreased.

The answer is it decreases.

15. _____

d. As a consequence of the output effect, what happens to the cost-minimizing combination of capital and labor?

The output effect indicates how the firm's choice of inputs is affected by the _____ in the level of

16. _____

17. _____

18. _____

19. _____

production. The level of output has decreased. If an input is _____ when the level of output decreases, the firm uses less; on the other hand if an input is inferior when the level of output decreases, the firm uses _____. Since labor is normal, less labor is used as a consequence of the output effect; since capital is inferior, _____ capital is used.

The answer is labor decreases and capital increases.

e. Accounting for both the substitution and output effects, what happens to the usage of labor and capital?

20. _____

21. _____

For labor the substitution and output effects work in the _____ direction causing the amount of labor used to decrease. For capital the substitution and output effects work in the same direction also causing the amount used to _____.

The answer is less labor used and more capital used.

3. Initially, the wage rate of labor is $5.00 and the rental rate of capital is $10.00. The firm is producing 1,000 units of output. The rental rate decreases from $10.00 to $8.00. Labor is a normal input; capital is inferior.

22. _____

a. What happens to the slope of the firm's equal cost curve?

23. _____

b. As a consequence of the substitution effect, what has happened to the cost-minimizing combination of labor and capital?

24. _____
25. _____

c. Typically what happens to the firm's marginal cost curve? What happens to its profit-maximizing level of output?

26. _____

d. As a consequence of the output effect what happens to the cost-minimizing combination of capital and labor?

27. _____

e. Accounting for both the substitution and output effects, what happens to the usage of labor and capital?

4. Initially, the wage rate of labor is $5.00 and the rental rate of capital is $10.00. The firm is producing 1,000 units of output. The wage rate decreases from $5.00 to $3.50. Labor and capital are normal inputs.

a. What happens to the slope of the firm's equal cost curve?

28. _____

b. As a consequence of the substitution effect, what has happened to the cost-minimizing combination of labor and capital?

29. _____

c. Typically what happens to the firm's marginal cost curve? What happens to its profit-maximizing level of output?

30. _____
31. _____

d. As a consequence of the output effect, what happens to the cost-minimizing combination of capital and labor?

32. _____

e. Accounting for both the substitution and output effects, what happens to the usage of labor and capital?

33. _____

5. Initially, the wage rate of labor is $5.00 and the rental rate of capital is $10.00. The firm is producing 1,000 units of output. The wage rate increases from $5.00 to $7.50. Labor is an inferior input; capital is normal.

a. What happens to the slope of the firm's equal cost curve?

34. _____

b. As a consequence of the substitution effect, what has happened to the cost-minimizing combination of labor and capital?

35. _____

c. Typically what happens to the firm's marginal cost curve? What happens to its profit-maximizing level of output?

36. _____
37. _____

d. As a consequence of the output effect what happens to the cost-minimizing combination of capital and labor?

38. _____

e. Accounting for both the substitution and output effects, what happens to the usage of labor and capital?

39. _____

PRICING OF LABOR

1. The labor market is competitive and the market for the good produced is competitive also. The price of the good produced has increased.

   a. What happens to the marginal physical product of labor curve?

   Nothing, the increase in the price of the good will _____ affect the marginal productivity of labor.

40. _____

   The answer is nothing.

   b. What happens to the marginal revenue product of labor curve?

   The marginal revenue product of labor equals the change in the firm's total revenues resulting from the employment of one additional unit of _____. When one additional unit of labor is hired, total output increases by an amount equal to the marginal _____ product of labor. Each additional unit of output increases total revenue by an amount equal to marginal _____. Consequently, marginal revenue product of labor equals marginal physical product of labor _____ marginal revenue. Since the market for the good being produced is competitive, marginal revenue will equal the _____ of the good. The higher price of the good will _____ marginal revenue causing the marginal revenue product of labor curve to shift _____ and to the right.

41. _____

42. _____

43. _____

44. _____

45. _____

46. _____

47. _____

The answer is it shifts up and to the right.

c. What happens to each individual firm's demand curve for labor? To the market demand curve for labor?

48. _____

49. _____

Each individual firm's demand curve for labor is its marginal _____ product of labor curve. Since each firm's marginal revenue product curve has shifted up and to the right, each firm's individual demand curve for labor will shift to the _____.

The answer is it shifts to the right.

50. _____

51. _____

The market demand curve for labor is the _____ sum of each firm's individual demand curve. Since each firm's individual demand curve shifts to the right, the market demand curve will shift to the _____ also.

The answer is it shifts to the right.

d. What happens to the supply curve for labor?

The increase in the price of the good being produced has no effect on the supply curve for labor.

The answer is nothing.

e. What happens to the equilibrium wage rate and quantity of labor?

52. _____

53. _____

The equilibrium wage rate and quantity of labor in a competitive labor market is determined by the _____ demand and supply curves for labor. The demand curve has shifted to the right and the supply curve is unchanged. The equilibrium wage rate and quantity will _____.

The answer is both increase.

2. The labor market is competitive and the market for the good produced is competitive also. Labor becomes more productive.

   a. What happens to the marginal physical product of labor curve?

54. _____

   b. What happens to the marginal revenue product of labor curve?

55. _____

   c. What happens to each individual firm's demand curve for labor? The market demand curve for labor?

56. _____
57. _____

   d. What happens to the supply curve for labor?

58. _____

   e. What happens to the equilibrium wage rate and quantity of labor?

59. _____

3. The labor market is competitive and the market for the good produced is competitive also. The supply of labor decreases.

   a. What happens to the marginal physical product of labor curve?

60. _____

   b. What happens to the marginal revenue product of labor curve?

61. _____

   c. What happens to each individual firm's demand curve for labor? The market demand curve for labor?

62. _____
63. _____

   d. What happens to the supply curve for labor?

64. _____

   e. What happens to the equilibrium wage rate and quantity of labor?

65. _____

4. The labor market is competitive and the market for the good produced is a monopoly. The monopolist's fixed costs increase.

   a. What happens to the marginal physical product of labor curve?

66. _____

67. _____

b. What happens to the marginal revenue product of labor curve?

c. What happens to each individual firm's demand curve for labor? The market demand curve for labor?

68. _____
69. _____

70. _____

d. What happens to the supply curve for labor?

e. What happens to the equilibrium wage rate and quantity of labor?

71. _____

5. The labor market is competitive and the market for the good produced is a monopoly. The monopolist's marginal revenues increase.

a. What happens to the marginal physical product of labor curve?

72. _____

b. What happens to the marginal revenue product of labor curve?

73. _____

c. What happens to each individual firm's demand curve for labor? The market demand curve for labor?

74. _____
75. _____

76. _____

d. What happens to the supply curve for labor?

e. What happens to the equilibrium wage rate and quantity of labor?

77. _____

EFFICIENCY

6. The rate of technical substitution for Firm X is 5 and that for Firm Y is 2.

a. From the information provided above can you determine if the economy is efficient from a technical, exchange, or output mix standpoint?

The relationship between the firm's rates of technical substitution determine whether or not the economy is

78. _____

79. _____

80. _____

_____ efficient. The relationship between the consumer's marginal rates of substitution determine whether or not the economy is efficient from the standpoint of _____. The relationship between the consumer's marginal rates of substitution and the rate of _____ transformation determine whether or not the economy is producing an efficient mix of output.

The answer is from the standpoint of production.

b. What does efficiency mean in this context?

81. _____

Technical efficiency refers to whether inputs could be reallocated between firms so as to _____ the production of one firm without reducing the production of the other firm.

The answer is inputs can be reallocated so as to increase the production of one firm without reducing the production of other firms.

c. Is the economy efficient in this context? What change would enhance efficiency?

82. _____

Since the rates of technical substitution are not equal, _____ results.

The answer is no.

83. _____

84. _____

85. _____

Since the rate of technical substitution for Firm X is 5, Firm X could produce the same amount of output by using one more unit of labor and _____ less units of capital. Similarly, Firm Y could produce the same amount of output by using one less unit of labor and _____ more units of capital. If Firm Y gives Firm X one unit of labor in exchange for three units of capital, both firms can produce _____ output.

The answer is Firm X should give labor to Firm Y in exchange for captial.

7. The rate of product transformation is 3 and marginal rate of substitution for Smith is 5.

   a. From the information provided above can you determine if the economy is efficient from a technical, exchange, or output mix standpoint?

      The relationship between the firm's rates of _____ substitution determine whether or not the economy is technically efficient. The relationship between the consumer's marginal rates of _____ determine whether or not the economy is efficient from the standpoint of exchange. The relationship between the consumer's marginal rates of substitution and the rate of product transformation determine whether or not the economy is producing an efficient _____ of output.

      The answer is from the standpoint of the output mix.

   b. What does efficiency mean in this context?

      An efficient mix of outputs refers to whether consumers could be made better off by the production of a different _____ of outputs.

      The answer is consumers can be made better off if a different output mix were produced.

   c. Is the economy efficient in this context? What change would enhance efficiency?

      Since the consumer's marginal rates of substitution do not equal the rate of product transformation, _____ results.

      The answer is no.

      Smith's marginal rate of substitution is 5; he is willing to forgo the consumption of _____ units of good Y in order to consume one additional unit of good X. Since the rate of product transformation is 3, one additional unit of good X could be produced at

86. _____

87. _____

88. _____

89. _____

90. _____

91. _____

- 301 -

92. _____   the sacrifice of only _____ units of good Y. More of good X should be produced.

The answer is produce more good X.

8. The marginal rate of substitution for Smith is 4 and that for Jones is 4 also.

     a. From the information provided above, can you determine if the economy is efficient from a technical, exchange, or output mix standpoint?

93. _____

94. _____   b. Is the economy efficient in this context?

9. The marginal rate of substitution for Smith is 3; the marginal rate of substitution for Jones is 6.

     a. From the information provided above can you determine if the economy is efficient from a technical, exchange, or output mix standpoint?

95. _____

96. _____   b. Is the economy efficient in this context?

10. The rate of technical substitution for Firm X is 2; the rate of technical substitution for Firm Y is 3.

     a. From the information provided above, can you determine if the economy is efficient from a technical, exchange, or output mix standpoint?

97. _____

98. _____   b. Is the economy efficient in this context?

11. The marginal rate of substitution for Smith is 4; the rate of product transformation is 8.

     a. From the information provided above can you determine if the economy is efficient from a technical, exchange, or output mix standpoint?

99. _____

100. _____   b. Is the economy efficient in this context?

ANSWERS

1. more
2. expensive
3. up
4. decreases
5. change
6. decreased
7. less
8. inferior
9. decrease
10. decrease
11. negative
12. more
13. constant
14. capital
15. up
16. change
17. normal
18. more
19. more
20. same
21. increase
22. more steeply sloped
23. less L, more K
24. shifts down
25. increases
26. more L, less K
27. both ambiguous
28. less steeply sloped
29. more L, less K
30. shifts up
31. decreases
32. more L, more K
33. More L, K ambiguous
34. more steeply sloped

35. less L, more K
36. shifts down
37. increases
38. more L, less K
39. both ambiguous
40. not
41. labor
42. physical
43. revenue
44. times
45. price
46. increase
47. up
48. revenue
49. right
50. horizontal
51. right
52. market
53. increase
54. shifts up and right
55. shifts up and right
56. shifts right
57. shifts right
58. nothing
59. both increase
60. nothing
61. nothing
62. nothing
63. nothing
64. shifts left
65. wage up, quantity down
66. nothing
67. nothing
68. nothing

69. nothing
70. nothing
71. nothing
72. nothing
73. shift up and right
74. shifts right
75. shifts right
76. nothing
77. both increase
78. technically
79. exchange
80. product
81. increase
82. inefficiency
83. five
84. two
85. more
86. technical
87. substitution
88. mix
89. mix
90. inefficiency
91. five
92. two
93. exchange
94. yes
95. exchange
96. no
97. technical
98. no
99. output mix
100. no